BRITAIN'S
COLD WAR HERITAGE

PETER ROBINSON & MILKA IVANOVA

AMBERLEY

ACKNOWLEDGEMENTS

We would like to thank all those who have helped put the book together and who have shared images, information and insight. In particular, for their generous sharing of images for the book:

Ryan Ellis (Royal Signals Museum)
Alan Rawsterne
Steve Parker (Military Vehicles Trust)
Wesley Perriman (British Nuclear Test Veterans Association)
Nigel Heaps MBE (*Exposure Magazine* and the British Nuclear Test Veterans Association)
Steve Bell (Norfolk and Suffolk Air Museum)
Dr Katherine Bedford (English Heritage)
Dr Hattie Hearne (Imperial War Museum)
RAF Radar Museum

First published 2025

Amberley Publishing
The Hill, Stroud
Gloucestershire, GL5 4EP

www.amberley-books.com

ISBN 978 1 3981 2145 4 (print)
ISBN 978 1 3981 2146 1 (ebook)

British Library Cataloguing in Publication Data.
A catalogue record for this book is available from the British Library.

Typesetting by SJmagic DESIGN SERVICES, India.
Printed in Great Britain.

Appointed GPSR EU Representative: Easy Access System Europe Oü, 16879218
Address: Mustamäe tee 50, 10621, Tallinn, Estonia
Contact Details: gpsr.requests@easproject.com, +358 40 500 3575

CONTENTS

INTRODUCTION

This book narrates Britain's Cold War through the rich heritage of this era. The chapters are organised to provide a chronology of the Cold War period, with key events, technologies and social impacts illustrated and explained through the many sites, collections and artefacts that are publicly accessible.

The book is the result of a research project funded by the British Academy at Leeds Beckett University. The project focused on exploring the visitor experience, curatorship, and memory associated with Cold War heritage in both Eastern and Western Europe. It is the first initiative of its kind, taking a tourism-oriented approach to Cold War heritage with the aim of promoting and raising awareness about sites and collections from this period. This, in turn, contributes to the preservation and restoration of this significant historical era.

The involvement of various research organisations in Cold War heritage indicates a renewed interest similar to the resurgence observed in industrial heritage during the 1980s. Through extensive research and engaging discussions with site owners, managers, curators, and volunteers, it became evident that opportunities for collaborative efforts exist. The creation of this book is one such collaborative endeavour intended to share Britain's Cold War history with a wider audience.

For further information, interested readers can visit www.coldwarnetwork.co.uk.

Entrance to the Holbeach ROC post.

1

POLITICAL IDEOLOGIES

The Cold War describes a period from the late 1940s to the early 1990s, a period of intense geopolitical tension and rivalry between, pejoratively, 'the West' (the US and Europe) and 'the East' (the former USSR and, to a lesser extent, China, though more recent research suggests there was a greater western concern in relation to China's potential influence and global reach). The period was the result of a broader ideological struggle between the United States and the Soviet Union, with both sides seeking to spread their respective political and economic systems and gain influence over other countries.

The battle-less battlefields of the Cold War were maintained through the escalation of technological and scientific development on both sides of the conflict, leading to an arms race that resulted in the proliferation of nuclear weapons. This almost guaranteed the mutually assured destruction of all participants if the war heated up.

Throughout the period, both the United States and the Soviet Union engaged in arms control negotiations to limit the proliferation of nuclear weapons and reduce tensions. Notable agreements include the Strategic Arms Limitation Talks (SALT), the Intermediate-Range Nuclear Forces (INF) Treaty, and the Strategic Arms Reduction Treaty (START). These agreements demonstrated a willingness on both sides to de-escalate the arms race and prioritise diplomacy over military confrontation.

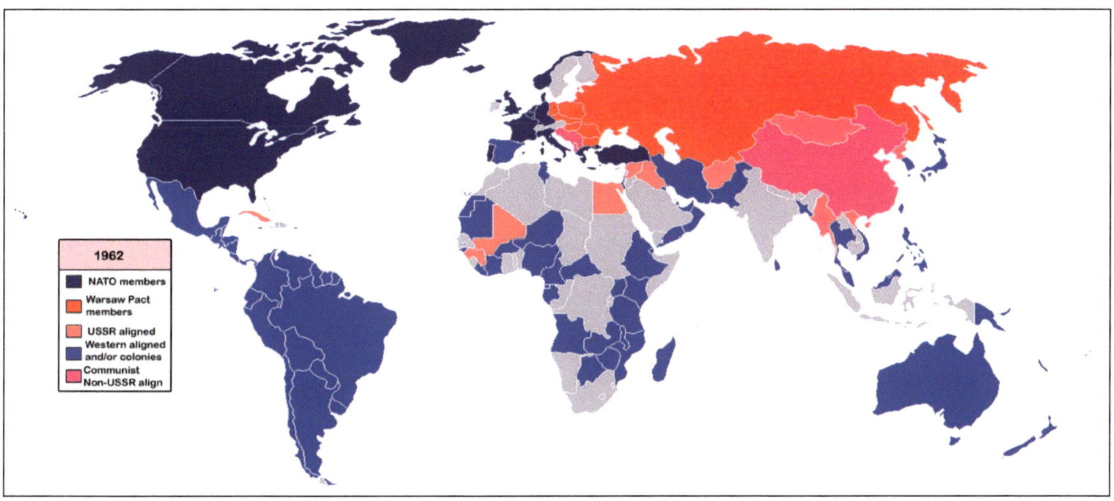

A politically divided world, 1953.

It is important to note, of course, that it was not the possession of a nuclear arsenal alone but the rapid development of technologies such as radar and the development of airspace-defence strategies that ensured each country would have time to launch a nuclear response had one side fired a nuclear missile. Consequently, mutually assured destruction was essentially the reason that the war remained one of political machinations, rhetoric, propaganda and intelligence gathering.

Mutually assured destruction.

2

THE EMERGING THREAT

On 6 August 1945, the US dropped a nuclear bomb on the Japanese city of Hiroshima. Three days later, a second bomb was dropped on the city of Nagasaki. (Both planes, the *Enola Gay* and the *Bockscar*, remain in preservation in US museums.) These events demonstrated the devastating power of nuclear weapons and led to a realisation that possession of nuclear weapons provided a significant strategic advantage.

In 1945, only the US possessed such weaponry. By 1945, the Soviet Union was developing its own nuclear missiles – the race for atomic supremacy had begun, contributing to a cycle of escalating tensions and mutual suspicion during the early years of the Cold War. Possession of such a powerful bomb also shaped the concept of deterrence theory, which suggests that possessing a significant nuclear arsenal acts as a deterrent, as the fear of

Hiroshima Peace Memorial.

mutually assured destruction would prevent either side from launching a first strike. The principle of deterrence became a key strategic doctrine during the Cold War.

In 1947, US President Harry S. Truman introduced the Truman Doctrine, which outlined the policy of containment and aimed to prevent the spread of communism by providing economic and military aid to countries facing communist insurgencies or pressure, such as Greece and Turkey. This policy set the stage for US intervention and involvement in various conflicts during the Cold War. It was followed, in 1948, by the Marshall Plan – a major economic aid programme to support the reconstruction of war-torn Europe. The plan aimed to stabilise and strengthen European economies and prevent the spread of communism by addressing the underlying economic and social conditions that could make countries vulnerable to Soviet influence.

In 1949, the North Atlantic Treaty Organization (NATO) was established as a collective defence alliance among Western democracies, including the United States and its European allies, as a direct response to the perceived threat posed by the Soviet Union. In response, the Eastern Bloc countries under Soviet influence formed the Warsaw Pact in 1955, creating a mirror image of military alliances.

3

GLOBAL PERSPECTIVES AND INFLUENTIAL MOMENTS

While this book focuses on Britain's Cold War, it is important to note that this was not a war fought in isolation and, as this book explains, the nation's relationship with the US shaped much of Britain's response, investment and military and civil defence strategies. While the war was largely cold, there were military flashpoints, some of which stretched over a significant period and others which represented the shift in ideological perspectives.

The Berlin Blockade and Airlift (1948–49)
The Soviet Union imposed a blockade on West Berlin in an attempt to gain control over the entire city. In response, the United States and its allies launched a major airlift operation to supply West Berlin, successfully breaking the blockade and ensuring the city's survival. A plane used during the airlift is part of the IWM collection at Duxford.

The Korean War (1950–53)
This began when North Korea, supported by the Soviet Union and China, invaded South Korea. The United Nations, with the United States leading a multinational force, intervened to support South Korea. The war ended in a stalemate and the division of Korea along the thirty-eighth parallel, which remains to this day.

US Navy R5D Skymasters at Tempelhof Airfield during the Berlin Airlift.

UN poster referring to the 'communist invasion' of South Korea.

The Cuban Missile Crisis (1962)

This was a tense standoff between the United States and the Soviet Union over the placement of Soviet nuclear missiles in Cuba. The crisis brought the world to the brink of nuclear war but was ultimately resolved through negotiations, with both sides agreeing to remove their missiles from Cuba and Turkey, respectively.

President John F. Kennedy meets with members of the Executive Committee of the National Security Council (EXCOMM) regarding the crisis in Cuba.

UH-1D helicopters in Vietnam, 1966.

The Vietnam War (1955–75)

This war was a protracted conflict between the communist forces of North Vietnam, supported by the Soviet Union and China, and the non-communist forces of South Vietnam, backed by the United States and its allies. The war ended in the victory of North Vietnam and the reunification of the country under communist rule.

The Soviet-Afghan War (1979–89)

This began when the Soviet Union invaded Afghanistan to support the communist government facing a growing insurgency. The United States, along with other Western countries, provided support to the Afghan resistance (Mujahideen) in their fight against Soviet forces. The war ended with the withdrawal of Soviet troops and the eventual collapse of the Soviet Union.

Additionally, there were several wars fought by proxy, with the US and the Soviet Union supporting different sides in the decolonisation of Africa through conflicts in Angola, Mozambique, Nicaragua (Central America) and in the Arab-Israeli conflicts in the Middle East.

Soldiers ride aboard a Soviet BMD airborne combat vehicle.

4

THE BEGINNING OF THE END

During a safety test on 26 April 1986 a series of errors and design flaws caused a reactor at the Chornobyl nuclear power station near Prypiat, Ukraine, to overheat and explode. The explosion released large quantities of radioactive material into the environment, leading to one of the worst nuclear disasters in history. The fire burned for days and the radioactive fallout spread over a wide area, contaminating the environment and causing long-term health effects for many people, including increased rates of cancer and other diseases. While the immediate impact was the loss of life and injuries to plant workers and the evacuation of nearby communities due to the high radiation levels, the disaster also exposed the flaws in the Soviet nuclear programme.

The disaster raised questions about governance, transparency, and safety standards. The mishandling of the accident and the initial cover-up damaged the credibility and legitimacy of the Soviet government, leading to a loss of trust among the Soviet people. It placed a significant economic strain on the state and created a long-term environment and health impacts that the already struggling economy was ill-placed to manage, revealing further economic inefficiencies and mismanagement, which had a profound impact on the international perception of the Soviet Union.

An abandoned building in Prypiat.

It sparked public activism and demands for reform and coincided with the leadership of Mikhail Gorbachev, who initiated policies of glasnost (openness) and perestroika (restructuring). The disaster contributed to the growing discontent in the Soviet Union and paved the way for reforms that ultimately led to its collapse and the end of the Cold War.

During this period, the East German government, under mounting economic and political challenges, was also facing growing internal discontent. The Soviet Union's weak economy and the economic disparity between East and West Germany, along with restrictions on freedom of speech and movement, led to increased demands for change. Peaceful demonstrations and mass protests demanding political reform and freedom began to escalate in East Germany in the late 1980s, and on 9 November 1989, the East German government announced that citizens could travel freely to West Germany. The announcement was intended to ease public pressure and respond to the demands for greater freedom. However, the government's decision was misinterpreted, leading to a rush of people gathering at the Berlin Wall, demanding to cross into West Berlin. The overwhelmed border guards eventually yielded, and the crossing points were opened, allowing thousands of people to pass through.

It marked a significant turning point in history, leading to the reunification of Germany in 1990 and the eventual end of the Cold War, with a wave of democratic revolutions sweeping across Eastern Europe, leading to the fall of communist regimes in countries such as Poland, Hungary, East Germany, Czechoslovakia, and Romania.

A preserved part of the Berlin Wall at Niederkirchnerstraße.

5

AN EMERGING LEGACY

In the UK, the Ministry of Defence's 1994 'Options for Change' initiative pinpointed over 100 surplus military and emergency establishments, including naval ports, nineteenth-century garrisons, ammunition plants, airstrips, and underground bunkers. The research also identified around 10,000 grid-referenced Cold War remains.

In the years that followed the end of the Cold War, a vast number of sites – encompassing military bases, clandestine factories, subterranean shelters, radar and surveillance stations, and missile research facilities – have been declassified. Some have morphed into tourist hotspots; a significant number have been razed; a few remain deserted, beckoning urban adventurers. There is also an expansive array of Cold War artefacts, including aircraft, missiles, radar, spy equipment, computing devices, communication tools, alert systems, and contemporary media. While a considerable volume of official documents, archives, and information was obliterated prior to the declassification of many sites, the surviving evidence of the period helps to tell Britain's Cold War story.

Sound mirrors at Romney Marsh, Kent, are some of the more accessible remains of Britain's acoustic early warning defence, which were superseded by the development of radar at Bawdsey and Orford Ness during the Cold War. (Image Dr Peter Robinson)

6

BRITAIN'S COLD WAR BEGINS

Britain had begun its development of nuclear weapons in the late 1940s because of the growing recognition among British policymakers that the international order had fundamentally changed, and new security challenges were emerging. Keen to maintain its status as a major global power, the possession of nuclear weapons was seen as a demonstration of technological prowess and military strength.

The United States, which had developed atomic bombs during the Second World War, was willing to share its nuclear technology and information with its closest allies. The close partnership with the United States in intelligence and military affairs led Britain to seek a nuclear deterrent with American support.

This allowed Britain to maintain its seat at the table of world powers, particularly at a time when the empire was undergoing decolonisation, and an independent deterrent would enable the country to preserve its autonomy and decision-making capabilities in international affairs. By developing its own nuclear weapons, Britain aimed to have an independent nuclear deterrent that it could control and deploy according to its national interests rather than relying solely on the protection and decisions of other nuclear-armed states.

In 1952, Britain successfully conducted its first nuclear weapons test, codenamed Operation Hurricane. This test marked the country's entry into the nuclear weapons club. The Blue Danube was a free-fall air-droppable nuclear fission gravity bomb that could

Blue Danube replica at The Gorse, Thetford (formerly RAF Barnham). (Dr Peter Robinson)

be deployed from an aircraft. It was a relatively simple design, utilising a nuclear core or warhead, conventional explosives, and a casing. The bomb was designed to be delivered to the target from one of the Royal Air Force's V-bombers and would detonate upon impact.

FISSION-BASED NUCLEAR BOMB

There are five stages to a fission-based bomb:

- Critical Mass: A fission-based nuclear bomb relies on the principle of achieving a critical mass of fissile material, such as enriched uranium-235 or plutonium-239. The critical mass is the minimum amount of fissile material required to sustain a self-sustaining chain reaction.
- Initiation: To initiate the nuclear explosion, a conventional explosive, such as TNT, is used to create a powerful shockwave that compresses the fissile material, bringing it closer to the critical mass.
- Neutron Generation: The compressed fissile material creates conditions that cause neutrons to be released from the material itself or from a neutron initiator. These neutrons then bombard the fissile material, increasing the chances of a nuclear chain reaction.
- Chain Reaction: When a sufficient number of neutrons are present, they collide with the atomic nuclei of the fissile material, causing them to split (fission) and release a tremendous amount of energy. This energy is released in the form of an explosion, along with the emission of additional neutrons.
- Energy Release: The energy released during the chain reaction creates an intense blast wave, heat, and a massive release of radiation, including gamma rays and neutron radiation.

Storage of the fissile core required very safe facilities. There were two key sites in the UK, one of which survives in its original layout at the former RAF Barnham in Thetford. The site was sold in 1966 to Keith Eldred and his wife, who quickly realised that the land they had acquired had something of a unique history. The site, now open to the public occasionally and better known as The Gorse Industrial Estate, comprises fifty-seven hutches for storing fissile cores, three storage facilities (one destroyed by fire) for the main bomb casings, a laboratory, fire station, guard house, security fencing and watchtowers. Designed as much for propaganda, the fifty-seven hutches would have created the illusion of a large stockpile of weapons when viewed from above, but in reality, there were rarely more than a handful of fissile cores stored at the site.

Above: Hutches for storing nuclear fissile cores at The Gorse Industrial Estate.

Right: Storage container inside the hutch.

7

RADAR SYSTEMS AND HOME CHAIN

In the 1930s, several British scientists and engineers worked on radar technology. Sir Robert Watson-Watt and his team at the Radio Research Station based at Bawdsey Manor on the Essex coast, later known as the Telecommunications Research Establishment, or TRE (now a PGL Holidays facility), conducted experiments to demonstrate the feasibility of detecting aircraft using radio waves. Early success led to the development of the Chain Home radar system, which consisted of a network of radar stations located along the coast, providing early warning of approaching enemy aircraft. Chain Home used large, fixed, and high-frequency radar antennas to detect and track aircraft over long distances.

Radar played a crucial role in the defence of Britain against German air attacks. The Chain Home system provided advanced warning of incoming Luftwaffe aircraft during

Bawdsey Manor. (John Fielding)

The Bawdsey Radar Block now houses the Bawdsey Radar Museum. (Dr Peter Robinson)

the Battle of Britain in 1940, allowing the Royal Air Force (RAF) to intercept and engage them effectively. Throughout the war, radar technology continued to evolve. British scientists and engineers developed new radar systems, such as the Chain Home Low (CHL) radar for low-level aircraft detection and the cavity magnetron, a key component for developing smaller and more effective radar systems.

Other systems developed in Britain included Airborne Interception Radar, which was developed to allow RAF night fighters to detect and intercept enemy aircraft during night-time operations (developed using Black Beacon at Orford Ness). Britain also developed ground-controlled interception, which worked in conjunction with the RAF's Fighter Command, providing real-time information and guidance to intercepting fighters, greatly improving their effectiveness and leading the Cold War-era development of systems including the Marconi Type 264 radar and the Ferranti Airpass radar. This provided enhanced capabilities for air defence and navigation.

The story of radar is recounted in the museum that is housed in the Bawdsey Radar Transmitter Block, though its development also encompasses the former RAF site at Orford Ness. Churchill saw the first radar in action at Orford.

Orford Ness was to go on to play an important role in radar development as the site for Cobra Mist, a classified radar project conducted by the United States Air Force (USAF) and

Chain Home Low radar at Hopton-on-Sea. Only one example of these masts survives and is now a listed structure at RAF Stenigot in Lincolnshire.

the RAF during the Cold War, which began in the 1960s to develop an over-the-horizon (OTHR) radar system capable of detecting and tracking ballistic missiles launched from the Soviet Union. The primary objective was to study the ionosphere, a region of the Earth's upper atmosphere, and its effect on the propagation of radio waves.

The facility at Orford Ness consisted of a large array of antenna towers and associated buildings. The system utilised a high-frequency (HF) band and bounced signals off the ionosphere to detect and track distant targets. It was intended to provide early warning of missile launches and contribute to the defence capabilities of the United States and its allies.

However, the project faced numerous technical challenges and operational issues. The complex nature of the ionosphere and the limitations of the HF band made it difficult to achieve consistent and accurate results. Despite ongoing efforts to improve the system, the project did not meet its original objectives and was eventually cancelled in 1973. There were also suspicions that its effectiveness was impeded by Russian shipping operations in the area that interfered with the signal. There were certainly stories of Russian ships disguised as fishing trawlers being used to observe activities at Orford.

The Cobra Mist site is adjacent to the area open to the public and owned by The National Trust, but the specifics of Cobra Mist and its exact capabilities remain classified.

The Cobra Mist site at Orford, adjacent to the National Trust site, which is open to the public. (Hohum)

Since 1963, RAF Fylingdales in North Yorkshire has played a pivotal role in providing an unceasing early warning service for ballistic missiles, jointly serving the UK and US governments. The iconic golf ball radomes were replaced in 1992 with the introduction of the Solid State Phased Array Radar, capable of monitoring a wide array of objects, including satellites and space debris, with remarkable precision, extending its reach some 3,000 miles into space. This complex operation is orchestrated by a dedicated workforce of approximately 320 individuals, composed of service personnel, Ministry of Defence Police, and civilian staff, who diligently man the site, safeguarding against potential threats under the UK Space Command.

Fylingdales Air Force Station. (Defense Visual Information Distribution Service)

8

AIR DEFENCE AND ROTOR

To use data from radar effectively, a series of radar stations were developed as part of the country's air defence system during the early Cold War period. These ROTOR stations were established to provide early warning and tracking of potential airborne threats, particularly Soviet bombers. The programme of works began in the early 1950s as an upgrade to the existing Chain Home and Chain Home Low radar systems.

Each ROTOR station consisted of a combination of radar installations, command centres, and support facilities. They were strategically located across the country, primarily along the coastlines, to monitor and protect against potential air attacks from over the sea and to provide an effective early warning system.

Some stations were developed in existing locations and on RAF bases, while others were installed in newly constructed underground bunkers, such as those at Hack Green and Kelvedon.

The radar systems used in the ROTOR stations were more advanced than their predecessors, employing new techniques such as pulse compression, which enhanced their ability to detect and track targets. The information gathered by the radar stations was then transmitted to regional control centres, which coordinated the response to any detected threats.

The ROTOR programme also included the development of the ROTOR Control and Reporting Centres (CRCs), which served as central command and control hubs for the radar network. They received radar data from multiple radar stations within their designated regions, processed the data, analysed it, and maintained a real-time picture of the airspace in their area of responsibility. At each CRC, trained operators and military personnel assessed the radar data to determine potential threats. They used various techniques, including comparing the radar tracks with flight plans and known aircraft identification codes, to identify and distinguish between friendly and hostile aircraft. The IFF system (Identification Friend or Foe) was used to identify friendly aircraft and distinguish them from potential threats. Friendly aircraft would emit a specific signal or respond to interrogation signals, indicating their friendly status.

When potential threats were identified, CRCs coordinated the response by alerting appropriate fighter squadrons and air defence units. They provided the necessary information to direct the interceptors toward the target, including the target's position, heading, and speed, while fighter aircraft, often stationed at airbases within the vicinity, were then scrambled to intercept and engage the identified hostile aircraft. Fighters deployed for this purpose were usually Gloster Meteors and Hawker Hunters.

Air Defence Operations Centres (ADOCs), such as the one that remains in situ and open to the public at the RFA Radar Museum (RAF Neatishead), are centralised command and control hubs for air defence operations within a specific region. They received information from multiple Control and Reporting Centres (CRCs), radar stations, and other intelligence sources, consolidating data to form a comprehensive situational awareness of the airspace. Their role was to maintain a real-time air situation display. Radar data from CRCs and other sources were fed into sophisticated display systems to create an accurate and up-to-date picture of the air activity in the region.

Trained operators and military personnel at the ADOCs assessed the radar data and other intelligence information to identify potential threats using the IFF system and other data. Threat assessments were made based on criteria such as the aircraft's trajectory, speed, altitude, and any suspicious or aggressive behaviour. This then enabled operators to make strategic decisions to respond to potential threats. They determined the appropriate course of action, considering factors such as the availability and readiness of interceptor aircraft, rules of engagement, and overall national defence priorities.

ADOCs were also responsible for directing interceptor aircraft to engage potential threats and providing guidance to interceptor pilots, including instructions on heading, altitude, and speed, to intercept and identify aircraft of interest. ADOCs maintained continuous communication with interceptor pilots to update them on the evolving situation and adjust their interception plans.

RAF Neatishead Cold War Operations Room. (The RAF Radar Museum)

To carry out this role effectively, ADOCs worked closely with various other agencies involved in air defence, including radar stations, CRCs, ground-based air defence systems, and higher-level command structures. They ensured effective coordination, information sharing, and integration of efforts to optimise the overall air defence response, disseminating information to relevant stakeholders, including higher-level command centres, government authorities, neighbouring air defence units, and fighter squadrons.

The ROTOR system was also complemented by ground-based air defence systems. This included anti-aircraft artillery, such as the Bofors 40mm gun and the 3.7-inch heavy anti-aircraft gun, which provided point defence against enemy aircraft that penetrated the radar coverage area.

Over time, the ROTOR system evolved, and subsequent phases (ROTOR 1, ROTOR 2, and ROTOR 3) introduced improvements in radar technology and operational procedures. However, by the late 1950s and early 1960s, advancements in missile technology and the growing threat of intercontinental ballistic missiles shifted the focus of the UK's air defence strategy.

With the introduction of new missile-based defence systems, such as the Nike Hercules and the Bloodhound missile systems, the ROTOR stations gradually became less prominent. Many were decommissioned or repurposed for other uses in subsequent years, while others were integrated into later air defence initiatives.

Above left: Bloodhound ground-to-air missile at the RAF Radar Museum.

Above right: Bloodhound ground-to-air missile at the Norfolk and Suffolk Air Museum.

9

THE BRITISH ARMY IN GERMANY

The presence of the British Army in Germany during the Cold War was a significant aspect of the larger NATO (North Atlantic Treaty Organization) strategy to counter the perceived threat posed by the Soviet Union and the Warsaw Pact countries in Europe. The British Army played a crucial role in this strategy, and its presence in Germany was part of a broader Western alliance effort to deter aggression from the East and defend Western Europe.

After the defeat of Nazi Germany in 1945, Germany was divided into four occupation zones controlled by the Allied powers: the United States, the Soviet Union, the United Kingdom, and France. Berlin, the capital, was also divided into four sectors. However, tensions quickly emerged between the Western Allies and the Soviet Union, leading to the beginning of the Cold War. The Soviet Union blockaded West Berlin in 1948, leading to the Berlin Airlift, a massive effort by Western Allies to supply the city with necessities. This event highlighted the deepening divisions between the East and the West.

In 1949, West Germany (the Federal Republic of Germany) and East Germany (the German Democratic Republic) were established as separate states. The border between them became a focal point of tension and division during the Cold War. The British Army maintained a significant presence in Germany as part of the British Army of the Rhine (BAOR). It was stationed in the British Zone of Occupation and played a key role in ensuring stability in the region. Their primary role was, like that of other NATO forces, to deter any potential Soviet aggression in Europe. The presence of Western forces, including the BAOR, was meant to make any Soviet invasion of Western Europe too costly to contemplate.

The presence of the British Army in Germany was a visible symbol of Western commitment to the defence of Europe during the Cold War. It remained a significant part of NATO's strategy until the end of the Cold War in the early 1990s when the geopolitical landscape in Europe began to shift dramatically with the collapse of the Soviet Union and the reunification of Germany. Subsequently, many British forces were withdrawn from Germany, reflecting the changing security environment in Europe.

The work of the British Army in Germany is captured through these archive images from the Royal Signals Museum.

BRIXMIS, short for 'British Commander-in-Chief's Mission to the Group Soviet Forces of Occupation in Germany', was a highly secretive British intelligence-gathering mission that operated in East Germany during the Cold War. BRIXMIS used various vehicles over the years to conduct its surveillance and reconnaissance operations behind the Iron

Corporals Stacey and Stanton are working on underground (UG) cables. The Royal Signals were responsible for the provision of communications on all Royal Air Force airfields overseas. 21st Signal Regiment supported the Royal Air Force in Germany and maintained 500 kilometres of multi-pair UG cable, 2,600 telephone installations, 120 intercommunications systems and many other types of equipment providing the complicated and essential communications of the Strike airbases.

A Terminal Equipment (TE) Technician Corporal lines up a Voice Frequency Telegraph Channel over a radio relay carrier system during a BRUIN exercise. The decision to field BRUIN was taken in 1964, but by utilising existing equipment and 'off the shelf' telecommunications components, it was in service in BAOR by 1967. A key advantage of BRUIN was that, for the first time, the main radio transmitters could be separated from the headquarters, thus reducing the chance of the HQ location being detected by the enemy. Visitors can get hands-on with BRUIN at the Royal Signals Museum on Blandford Camp.

Curtain. The mission spanned several decades, and its vehicles evolved with changing technology and requirements. They were civilian vehicles that did not draw attention, such as standard sedans and station wagons. These vehicles were often equipped with hidden cameras and listening devices for covert surveillance. During the 1950s and 1960s, BRIXMIS started using specially modified cars based on the British Bristol 400 series. These cars were fitted with advanced surveillance equipment and communication devices. They were more sophisticated and purpose-built for intelligence gathering. Between the 1960s and 1980s, Land Rovers became the vehicle of choice. They were robust, versatile, and capable of handling the rough terrain of East Germany. As technology advanced, BRIXMIS vehicles continued to evolve. They became equipped with more sophisticated surveillance equipment, including improved cameras and communication systems.

BRIXMIS played a crucial role in gathering intelligence on Soviet and East German military activities during the Cold War. The mission's vehicles were an essential part of its operations, allowing BRIXMIS personnel to discreetly observe and document activities on the other side of the Iron Curtain. Today, BRIXMIS is remembered as one of the most secretive and successful intelligence missions of the Cold War, and its cars are a symbol of its covert operations behind enemy lines.

The sole surviving BRIXMIS G-Wagen is at the Military Intelligence Museum, while the only BRIXMIS Opel Senator is at RAF Cosford in the National Cold War Exhibition.

BRIXMIS Senator stuck on the TAC route.

10

V-BOMBERS AND COLD WAR JETS

In the early 1950s, the United Kingdom recognised the need for a strategic nuclear bomber force to deter potential adversaries and maintain its global influence. As a result, the British government issued a requirement for a new class of high-performance bombers capable of delivering nuclear weapons – in particular, the Blue Danube, which was being developed alongside the V-bomber project.

Each of the three major plane manufacturers in the UK – Vickers, Handley Page and Avro – were asked to develop a solution. Each was responsible for their bomber's design, development, and production.

The V-bomber programme represented a significant undertaking for the UK aviation industry, requiring extensive technological advancements and significant investment.

The National Cold War Collection at RAF Cosford.

The collaboration among the three manufacturers allowed for different approaches to be explored and brought together expertise from different design teams.

The Vickers Valiant was the first of the three to be developed. It made its maiden flight in 1951 and entered operational service with the Royal Air Force (RAF) in 1955. The Valiant was a high-wing monoplane with four engines, known for its distinctive crescent-shaped wings and was capable of delivering nuclear weapons as well as conventional bombs.

Handley Page developed the Victor bomber, which featured a unique crescent-shaped wing design and a large bomb bay capable of carrying a significant payload. It was designed for high-altitude strategic bombing and had in-flight refuelling capability. It first flew in 1952 and entered RAF service in 1957.

Avro was responsible for the development of the Vulcan, which became the most iconic and widely recognised V-bomber. The Vulcan featured a delta wing design and was known for its distinctive shape. It was designed to deliver nuclear weapons and had the capability to fly at high altitudes and high subsonic speed to deliver nuclear weapons deep into enemy territory. It was the last V-bomber to be developed and conducted its maiden flight in 1952 before entering operational service in 1956.

BRITISH AEROSPACE (BAE)

During the Cold War, BAE Systems, known as British Aerospace (BAE) at the time, played a significant role in the defence and aerospace industries, contributing to the defence capabilities of the United Kingdom and its allies. BAE Systems was involved in various aspects of the Cold War effort. Much of this work was undertaken at Filton, where the Bristol Aerospace Company, a key player in the development of Concorde, was subsumed into BAE.

They were involved in the production of aircraft such as the Harrier Jump Jet and the Tornado. These aircraft played crucial roles in the defence strategies of the UK and its NATO allies. They developed and manufactured missile systems, including air-to-air and surface-to-air missiles, including the Bloodhound, and, elsewhere, were involved in the construction of naval vessels, including submarines, frigates, and destroyers. The Royal Navy's nuclear submarines, armed with Trident nuclear missiles, were a key component of the UK's nuclear deterrent strategy.

BAE Harrier.

The Filton site, under both the Bristol Aerospace Company and BAE, secured contracts for work on both UK jets, including the Vulcan, and for also servicing US jets and designing and developing new systems for US hardware, given the lower cost of managing these aircraft in the UK rather than returning them to the US for upgrades. This was particularly important during the 1970s when the Filton site was, post-Concorde, short of contracts.

Work was mainly focussed on the F-111F, a versatile variable-geometry strike aircraft and a highly valuable asset for the US Air Forces in Europe, which had started arriving at the Suffolk airfield the previous year, as well as the F-111Es, which were stationed at Upper Heyford.

BAE hangars at Filton, close to the Bristol Aerospace Museum.

Over the years, the V-bombers underwent several upgrades and modifications to improve their performance and extend their operational lifespan. These included engine upgrades, avionics improvements, and weapon system enhancements.

The V-bombers formed the backbone of the RAF's strategic nuclear deterrent during the late 1950s and throughout the 1960s. They were stationed at several airbases in the UK, including RAF Waddington, RAF Scampton, and RAF Finningley, and were on standby to respond to potential nuclear threats. Their presence served as a deterrent against aggression.

VICTOR ALERT

'Victor Alert' refers to a state of readiness and readiness posture maintained by the Royal Air Force (RAF) during the Cold War and was associated with the Handley Page Victor strategic bombers. When the Victor bombers were on Victor Alert, they were fully armed, fuelled, and ready to be launched within a short period. The aircraft would be loaded with nuclear weapons and kept in a state of readiness, often positioned at dispersal airfields or other designated sites. This allowed for a rapid response and the ability to quickly deploy the bombers to their designated targets/if required.

The purpose of maintaining Victor Alert was to deter potential adversaries, ensure a swift and effective response in case of an attack, and demonstrate the UK's commitment to its nuclear deterrent capabilities. The readiness posture of the Victor bombers during the Victor Alert was a crucial aspect of the UK's overall nuclear deterrence strategy during the Cold War.

Victor Alert at RAF Upper Heyford. (Combined Military Service Digital Photographic Files)

As technology advanced, the V-bombers' capabilities became less relevant, and their operational roles shifted. The Valiant was the first to be retired in 1965. The Vulcan continued to serve in various roles, including conventional bombing and aerial refuelling, until its retirement in 1984. During the Falklands War in 1982, both the Vulcan and the Victor played important roles in supporting the British military operations.

On 30 April 1982, Operation Black Buck was launched, involving a series of long-range missions by Vulcans from Ascension Island in the Atlantic Ocean. The Vulcans, which

Vulcan Bomber in the National Cold War Collection at the RAF Museum, Cosford.

had been modified to carry out long-range precision bombing raids, were refuelled several times in the air by Victor tanker aircraft to extend their range (as were Harrier Jump Jets to support intelligence gathering and ground troops). During the Black Buck raids, the Vulcans carried conventional bombs, including 1,000-pound bombs and runway-cratering bombs. Their objective was to neutralise the airfield, denying the Argentine air force the ability to operate effectively from the Falklands.

Although the Vulcan missions did not cause significant physical damage to the runway, they succeeded in diverting Argentine resources and shifting their attention from other British operations. The psychological impact of the Vulcan raids on the Argentine forces was substantial.

The development of the V-bombers showcased British innovation and technological prowess during the Cold War, left a lasting legacy in the history of British aviation and served as a testament to the nation's commitment to maintaining a credible nuclear deterrent. The Vulcan, in particular, gained renewed popularity in later years and has become an iconic symbol of British aviation.

VULCAN TO THE SKIES

The 'Vulcan to the Skies' project was a British initiative that aimed to restore and preserve one Avro Vulcan and return it to flight. Vulcan XH558, which had been retired from RAF service in 1984, was chosen as the restoration candidate. Led by a team of dedicated engineers, technicians, and aviation enthusiasts, the restoration work took place at Bruntingthorpe Airfield in Leicestershire, England.

The restoration process was extensive and challenging. The project required sourcing or manufacturing various components, conducting structural repairs, and ensuring compliance with modern aviation regulations. Funding was primarily generated through public donations, sponsorship, and support from aviation enthusiasts.

After years of dedicated effort, the Avro Vulcan XH558 successfully made its first post-restoration flight on 18 October 2007. The aircraft was subsequently operated as part of the Vulcan Display Flight, performing airshows and public displays across the United Kingdom and abroad. It became a popular sight at airshows and events, captivating audiences with its distinctive appearance and powerful displays.

In 2015, after several years of flying displays, the XH558 made its final flight and was retired from active service once again. Since then, the project has transitioned into a preservation and educational initiative focused on maintaining the aircraft in ground-running condition and preserving its heritage for future generations.

Vulcan Bomber and Canberra.

Alongside the V-bomber force, the UK employed a number of other jets which can be seen in museum collections across the UK, including:

- The English Electric Canberra was a jet-powered light bomber and reconnaissance aircraft that served as a nuclear strike platform and was also used for photo reconnaissance and electronic warfare.
- The Blackburn Buccaneer was a low-level strike aircraft primarily used by the Royal Air Force and designed to operate from aircraft carriers to perform roles including nuclear strike, anti-ship operations, and precision bombing.

- The Hawker Hunter was a versatile jet fighter aircraft used by the RAF and others, entering service in the early 1950s and known for its agility and performance. The Hunter served in various roles, including air defence, ground attack, and reconnaissance.
- English Electric Lightning was a supersonic interceptor aircraft operated by the RAF. It entered service in the 1960s and was renowned for its exceptional speed and climb rate, designed to intercept and destroy enemy aircraft at high altitudes. The jet played a crucial role in defending UK airspace.
- The BAC Jet Provost was a training and light attack aircraft used by the RAF that served as a basic and advanced jet trainer for pilots transitioning to fast jet aircraft.
- The Panavia Tornado was a multi-role combat aircraft jointly developed by the United Kingdom, Germany, and Italy. The Tornado entered service in the late 1970s and played a prominent role in the RAF, which was designed for ground attack, air defence, and reconnaissance.
- The Gloster Meteor, introduced during the Second World War, became one of the world's first operational jet-powered fighter planes and played a significant role in post-war aviation development.

Left: English Electric Lightning at the Norfolk and Suffolk Air Museum.

Below: A collection of Cold War jets at the Norfolk and Suffolk Air Museum.

11

SPACE MONKEYS AND OTHER STORIES

During the Cold War, the secrecy surrounding military operations and political tensions between the East and West gave rise to various rumours and speculations in the UK. While it's important to note that rumours are often unsubstantiated and can vary widely, here are a few examples of the types of rumours that circulated during that time. Some, it turned out, were more accurate than others...

There were rumours that in the event of a nuclear war, designated safe areas or bunkers existed for government officials and elite individuals, while the general public would be left unprotected. Speculation surrounded the existence of secret underground bunkers and tunnels across the country, where government officials and military personnel could seek shelter in the event of an attack. There was indeed a network of bunkers. The construction of the secret bunker at Kelvedon was, locally at least, a poorly kept secret, with locals directing lost lorry drivers to the secret nuclear bunker they knew about.

The presence of intelligence agencies like MI5 and MI6 during the Cold War era led to rumours of widespread surveillance, infiltration, and espionage. It was speculated that anyone could be a spy or informant, creating an atmosphere of suspicion and paranoia. Some rumours suggested that the government was actively hiding information and engaging in cover-ups related to military activities, nuclear weapons, or other sensitive matters. These rumours often fuelled conspiracy theories and distrust in official narratives.

There were also rumours surrounding specific locations. The missile storage facility at RAF Barnham was lit by floodlights twenty-four hours a day, leading some locals to speculate the site was being used to train monkeys to go into space. Concerns about nuclear accidents or near-miss incidents involving nuclear weapons were widespread.

The secrecy surrounding military aircraft and experimental technology led to rumours of unidentified flying objects (UFOs) being linked to secret military operations. Sightings of unusual aerial phenomena were sometimes attributed to covert military activities. Rendlesham Forest, close to Orford Ness, Bawdsey, RAF Woodbridge and Bentwaters, was considered a hotspot of UFO sightings in the UK.

RENDLESHAM FOREST UFO SIGHTINGS

Rendlesham Forest, located in Suffolk, England, gained notoriety for a series of reported UFO sightings that occurred in late December 1980. This incident, often referred to as the 'Rendlesham Forest Incident' or the 'British Roswell', took place during the Cold War era and attracted significant attention from both military personnel and UFO enthusiasts.

The incident began on the night of 26 December 1980, when personnel from the United States Air Force (USAF) stationed at the nearby RAF Woodbridge base reported strange lights in the forest. Witnesses described seeing a series of unidentified objects in the sky, including a triangular-shaped craft with flashing lights and beams of light descending into the forest. The sightings continued over the next few nights, involving multiple witnesses, including military personnel and security personnel from the base.

The incident gained further attention when Lieutenant Colonel Charles Halt, the Deputy Base Commander at RAF Woodbridge, conducted an investigation and recorded his observations on an audio tape. In the recording, Halt describes witnessing strange lights, beams of light, and radiation readings in the forest. The incident remains one of the most famous UFO cases in the UK and has been the subject of numerous investigations, debates, and conspiracy theories.

Despite extensive investigations by both the UK and US military, no definitive explanation for the Rendlesham Forest Incident has been reached. Various theories have been proposed, ranging from misidentifications of mundane objects to extraterrestrial visitations. The incident continues to captivate the public's imagination and remains an intriguing part of the UFO lore associated with the Cold War era.

12

RESEARCH AND DEVELOPMENT

The Atomic Weapons Research Establishment (AWRE) was a British research facility located in Aldermaston, Berkshire. It was established in 1946 to centralise research and development efforts related to atomic weapons and nuclear energy.

During the Cold War, AWRE was primarily responsible for designing, developing, and testing nuclear weapons, as well as conducting research on the effects of nuclear explosions. It played a key role in developing the UK's first atomic bomb, which was successfully tested in 1952 as part of Operation Hurricane.

Operation Hurricane: British nuclear tests at Montebello Islands on 3 October 1952. Britain's first atomic weapon was detonated at 0800 hours.

Orford Ness, located on the Suffolk coast in England, was closely associated with AWRE during the Cold War. It was a remote and isolated peninsula that housed a top-secret radar research establishment. Orford Ness played a significant role in intelligence gathering and monitoring Soviet activities, particularly in relation to radar systems.

The location of Orford Ness was strategically chosen due to its proximity to the North Sea, which provided an excellent vantage point for monitoring Soviet activities. The site operated under high security, and access was strictly controlled. Much like AWRE, Orford Ness was shrouded in secrecy, and its true purpose remained unknown to the general public for many years.

The research conducted at AWRE advanced the UK's nuclear capabilities, contributing to the overall deterrence strategy of the Western bloc. Meanwhile, the monitoring and intelligence gathering at Orford Ness provided crucial insights into Soviet military activities, enhancing the West's situational awareness.

Today, AWRE has undergone several transformations and is now known as AWE (Atomic Weapons Establishment). It continues to be responsible for the design, manufacture, and support of nuclear warheads for the United Kingdom's defence programme. Orford Ness, on the other hand, is now a nature reserve and protected area managed by the National Trust, but remnants of its Cold War past can still be seen, serving as a reminder of the significant role it played during that era.

13

RACE TO THE STARS

The space race, which began in the late 1950s and continued into the 1970s, was fuelled by the same political and ideological tensions between the two superpowers. The launch of the Soviet satellite Sputnik 1 in October 1957 gave the Soviet Union an early advantage and shocked the United States. This event prompted the US government to invest heavily in its space programme and led to the creation of NASA (National Aeronautics and Space Administration) in 1958.

The race intensified with subsequent milestones. In April 1961, Soviet cosmonaut Yuri Gagarin became the first human to orbit the Earth, further increasing Soviet prestige. The United States responded with the ambitious goal of landing astronauts on the Moon. In 1969, NASA achieved this feat with the Apollo 11 mission, when American astronauts Neil Armstrong and Buzz Aldrin became the first humans to set foot on the lunar surface.

Throughout the space race, both nations competed to achieve various other milestones. These included the first woman in space (Valentina Tereshkova, Soviet Union, 1963), the first spacewalk (Alexei Leonov, Soviet Union, 1965), and the first space station (Salyut 1, Soviet Union, 1971). The development of new technologies, such as powerful rockets, advanced spacecraft, and life support systems, became essential in achieving these milestones.

The space race served as a symbolic battleground for the broader Cold War conflict. It represented a competition between the capitalist and communist systems, with each nation aiming to showcase its technological and scientific prowess. The accomplishments in space exploration had significant propaganda value, demonstrating the technological capabilities and ideological superiority of the respective nations.

During this period, Britain had its own space and rocket programme. However, it was relatively modest compared to those of the United States and the Soviet Union. The British space and rocket programme primarily focused on developing satellite technology and launching scientific missions.

Black Arrow was a British satellite launch vehicle developed in the 1960s and 1970s. Its purpose was to place small scientific and communication satellites into orbit. The Black Knight rockets were developed at Highdown above The Needles (Isle of Wight), allowing scientists and engineers to gather valuable data on various aspects of rocket technology, atmospheric research, and space exploration. The Needles site (now National Trust) provided a suitable location for rocket testing due to its coastal position, which facilitated safety measures and enabled rockets to be launched over the sea. The area's isolation also helped mitigate potential risks associated with rocket launches.

Above: Rocket testing site at High Down, Isle of Wight. The rockets were held down by gantries while their engines were fired. Test launching took place at Woomera in Australia. (Peter Trimming, CC BY-SA 2.0)

Left: A Black Arrow launch vehicle in the rocket park at Woomera, similar to the one that launched the UK's first satellite in 1971. (artq55, CC BY-SA 2.0)

The programme had a successful launch in 1970, placing the Prospero satellite, the first and only British satellite to be launched by a British rocket, into orbit. Other rocket-related activities and experiments were conducted at the Needles. These included testing of solid-fuel rocket motors, sounding rocket experiments, and research on rocket systems and components.

Another significant project was the Blue Streak missile programme. Originally developed as an intercontinental ballistic missile (ICBM) for the British military, the Blue Streak was later repurposed for satellite launches. However, the programme faced technical challenges and was eventually cancelled in 1972 before any satellite launches could take place.

The British space programme was further consolidated with the formation of the British National Space Centre (BNSC) in 1985. The BNSC aimed to coordinate and support Britain's space activities, including research, development, and international collaborations. It played a role in promoting British participation in European space projects, such as the European Space Agency (ESA).

While the space race tapered off in the 1970s, its legacy in space exploration and technological advancements remains significant, delivering advancements in rocketry and the establishment of long-lasting space programmes that continue to explore the cosmos to this day.

One of the rocket-firing stands for the Blue Streak missile at RAF Spadeadam.

Goonhilly Satellite Earth Station

Established in 1962, Goonhilly was designed to track and communicate with early satellites, including those from the United States and the Soviet Union. Its strategic location in south-west England made it an ideal site for receiving and transmitting signals from various satellites in orbit. Goonhilly had a collection of large parabolic dish antennas, with the iconic 'Arthur' being the largest of them all.

During the Cold War era, Goonhilly played a crucial role in supporting space missions and satellite communications. It received and transmitted signals for significant events such as the Apollo moon landings, providing a vital communication link between astronauts on the Moon and mission control centres. The station also contributed to tracking Soviet satellites and monitoring their activities, providing valuable intelligence to Western powers.

In addition to its role in space exploration and surveillance, Goonhilly served as a key international communications hub. It facilitated global telecommunication services, including telephone calls, television broadcasts, and data transmissions. The station's capabilities in satellite communications were continuously upgraded to keep up with advancements in technology and the increasing demands of the telecommunications industry.

Over the years, Goonhilly has evolved and adapted to changing technologies and communication needs. It has played a role in various satellite projects, including the European Space Agency's (ESA) missions. In recent years, the site has transformed into a space science and technology park, hosting companies and organisations involved in satellite operations, space research, and telecommunications.

Goonhilly remains an iconic symbol of Britain's contributions to space exploration and satellite communications. It stands as a testament to the country's technical expertise and its role in global telecommunications networks, leaving a lasting legacy in the field of satellite communications and the Cold War-era space race.

14

CIVIL DEFENCE AND THE ROYAL OBSERVER CORPS

In addition to their military defence function, ROTOR stations played a role in civil defence efforts because of the genuine fear of nuclear attacks. They served as a part of the civil defence warning system and were responsible for providing early warning of potential nuclear attacks, allowing authorities to initiate civil defence procedures. These procedures included sounding air-raid sirens, issuing warnings to the public, and initiating evacuation plans if necessary.

In the 1960s, the ROTOR system became outdated with the emergence of more advanced radar technology. As a result, ROTOR stations were gradually replaced by a new radar system called the Linesman/Mediator System. This system incorporated improved radar technology and communication systems, providing enhanced surveillance capabilities.

The entrance and guard house to Kelvedon Hatch Nuclear Bunker.

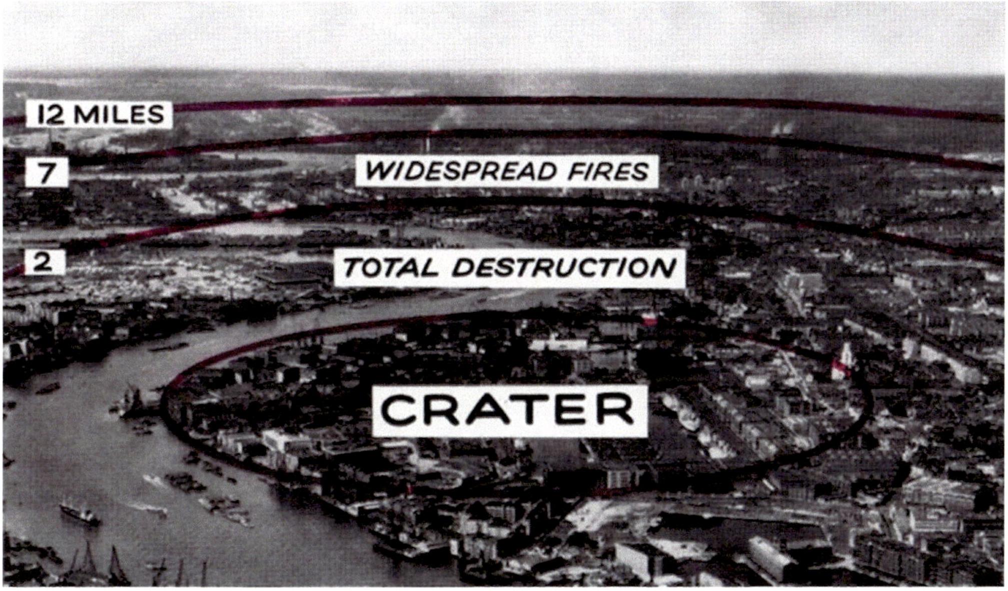

A Civil Defence poster showing the potential impact of a nuclear warhead on London.

ROC display at Norfolk and Suffolk Air Museum.

Throughout the 1960s and 1970s, the majority of the ROTOR stations were decommissioned and closed, though some were repurposed for other military and civilian uses, while others were abandoned or demolished. Those that were repurposed were often developed to serve as Emergency Government Centres or Regional Government Headquarters.

These facilities were intended to serve as command-and-control centres in the event of a nuclear war or national emergency. They would house government officials and provide

Barnton Quarry Operations Room under restoration.

a secure location for coordination and decision-making. They became part of the civil defence network. The ROC (Royal Observer Corps) was also integrated into the UK's civil defence system and worked closely with other organisations, such as the Home Office and the military.

Civil defence authorities were also tasked with pinpointing secure facilities for essential regional personnel. Among the chosen sites in the North East were Durham Prison, The Imperial Hotel in Blackpool, Scarborough's Grand Hotel, Arundel Castle, Craiglands Hotel in Ilkley, and Welbeck Abbey. The establishment of regional control centres with regional commissioners would have been imperative had London been targeted by nuclear missiles.

The ROC was a civilian volunteer organisation established in the United Kingdom in 1925. It played a crucial role in monitoring and reporting on aircraft movements and potential nuclear attacks during the Cold War. It was formed as a successor to the Air Raid Precautions (ARP) organisation, and its primary purpose was to provide visual and auditory observation of the skies to detect and report enemy aircraft during wartime. During the Cold War era, the ROC's role expanded to include monitoring and reporting on potential nuclear attacks. In the event of a nuclear strike, ROC posts across the country would be responsible for detecting and reporting the location, size, and nature of the blast.

Civil Defence poster explaining the hydrogen bomb and civil defence. (Crown Copyright)

York Cold War bunker.

At its peak, the ROC had a network of over 1,500 observation posts spread across the United Kingdom. These observation posts were strategically located to provide comprehensive coverage of the country's airspace. The posts were typically small, underground structures manned by trained volunteers who observed the skies and reported any aircraft sightings or other relevant information.

Monitoring centres, like York's Cold War Bunker, served as regional hubs for the ROC's operations. They were responsible for receiving, analysing, and disseminating information collected by the observation posts within their respective regions. The centres acted as communication and coordination centres, ensuring an efficient flow of information between the observation posts and the appropriate authorities, including other civil defence organisations, military units, and government agencies involved in national security and emergency response. They were also typically located in underground bunkers or hardened structures designed to provide protection against potential nuclear attacks or other threats.

Each monitoring centre had a dedicated team of trained personnel responsible for the management and operation of the centre. The staff included ROC officers and trained volunteers who were knowledgeable in the processes of data collection, analysis, and reporting. They were equipped with telecommunication equipment, such as radios, telephones, and telex machines, enabling communication with the observation posts and other relevant parties.

After the disbandment of the ROC in 1995, many of the observation posts were decommissioned, abandoned, or repurposed for other uses. Some former ROC posts have been preserved as historical sites or converted into museums, allowing visitors to learn about the role of the ROC in civil defence and national security during the Cold War era.

The legacy of the Royal Observer Corps remains significant, as its volunteers played a vital role in the defence and monitoring of the UK's airspace during the Second World War and the Cold War. Their dedication and service contributed to national security efforts and provided valuable insights into potential threats.

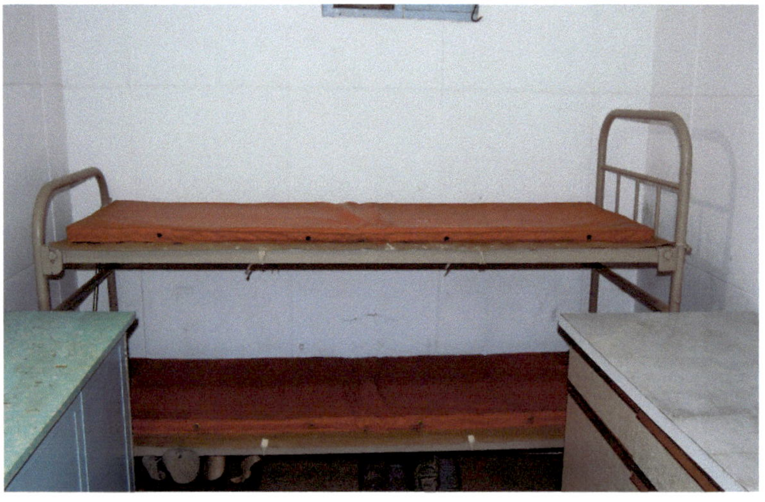

Sleeping space at ROC Holbeach.

15

US OPERATIONS ON UK SOIL

The UK and US have a long-established history of working in partnership. During the Cold War, several US operations took place on UK soil as part of the close military alliance between the United States and the United Kingdom, which included the establishment of multiple airbases on UK soil.

Both nations regularly conducted joint military exercises and training programmes on UK soil. These exercises aimed to enhance interoperability between the two militaries and improve their readiness to respond to potential threats. They involved land, air, and naval forces and often simulated various scenarios related to Cold War tensions.

On 16 May 1951, jurisdiction over several RAF bases – including RAF Bassingbourn, RAF Lakenheath, RAF Lindholme, RAF Manston, RAF Marham, RAF Mildenhall, RAF Sculthorpe, RAF West Drayton, and RAF Waddington – were transferred from the Third Air Force to the 7th Air Division.

British bases after the Second World War were not really capable of handling larger US planes, so new bases – including RAF Brize Norton, RAF Upper Heyford, RAF Fairford, and RAF Greenham Common – were established and began operation in 1952. Initially under RAF control, these bases were handed over to the USAF in 1951 but retained their RAF station designation, with both the RAF Ensign and the United States flag flown.

Propeller-driven B-29s and B-50s were replaced by Boeing B-47 Stratojets in 1953 and deployed to English bases. These deployments were initially part of temporary duty postings (TDY) involving a full wing of B-47s and KC-97 Stratofreighter refuelling tankers held in readiness for ninety days at an English base. In 1958, TDY postings gave way to the Reflex system, establishing a permanent SAC presence. A SAC airbase group was permanently assigned to each base, and the ninety-day deployments were replaced by twenty-one-day rotations of two or three aircraft with crews. These aircraft were maintained on full alert, ready to take off within fifteen minutes, armed with a Mk 39 nuclear bomb.

SAC B-47s in the UK were on alert during critical events like the Berlin Crisis of 1961 and the Cuban Missile Crisis. Thor missiles, manned by RAF units but controlled by SAC officers through a dual key system, were also on alert.

As intercontinental ballistic missiles and long-range B-52 Stratofortress bombers were introduced, SAC no longer required UK bases. Reflex deployments ceased in 1965, but the UK continued to be visited by SAC bombers, Lockheed U-2, and Lockheed SR-71 Blackbird reconnaissance aircraft.

Left: An aerial view of a portion of the base, showing a housing area in the foreground. The 20th Tactical Fighter Wing, US Air Force Europe (USAFE) and the 42nd Electronic Combat Squadron, USAFE, at Upper Heyford.

Below: Stratofortress at a UK airshow.

ABLE ARCHER 83

Exercise Able Archer 83 was a large-scale NATO military exercise that took place in November 1983. It was a particularly significant exercise as it occurred during a period of heightened tension between NATO and the Soviet Union. The exercise simulated a NATO nuclear release and involved the participation of NATO member countries, including the United States and the United Kingdom.

Able Archer 83 was designed to test and improve NATO's command and control procedures, particularly in the event of a nuclear conflict. It aimed to simulate realistic scenarios and assess the alliance's ability to respond effectively to a Soviet attack.

However, the exercise caused considerable concern and alarm within the Soviet Union. The Soviet leadership, already suspicious of NATO's intentions, misinterpreted some of the exercise's elements as a potential cover for a real surprise nuclear attack. The scale and intensity of Able Archer 83, combined with other factors such as heightened rhetoric and tensions during the period, fuelled Soviet fears of an imminent conflict.

The Soviet Union responded to the exercise by increasing its own military readiness and putting its own forces on high alert. The situation became highly tense, with both sides perceiving an increased risk of a nuclear war. Fortunately, cooler heads prevailed, and the tensions eventually subsided without escalating into a direct military confrontation.

Able Archer 83 served as a stark reminder of the potential dangers and misunderstandings that existed between NATO and the Soviet Union during the Cold War. It highlighted the need for improved communication and diplomatic efforts to prevent a potential miscalculation or accidental escalation of hostilities. The event also served as a catalyst for subsequent arms control negotiations between the two superpowers, such as the Intermediate-Range Nuclear Forces Treaty (INF Treaty), signed in 1987, which aimed to reduce the risk of nuclear war in Europe.

Volunteers at The RAF Radar Museum tell the story of Able Archer 83 in the control room used for the exercise.

In 1969, negotiations commenced between the US government and the UK to establish a base for the Lockheed SR-71 Blackbird aircraft. An agreement was reached in 1970, leading to the construction of a dedicated SR-71 hangar at RAF Mildenhall.

SAC tanker aircraft, including Boeing KC-135 Stratotankers and McDonnell Douglas KC-10 Extenders based in the UK, supported missions like the 1980 hostage rescue attempt in Iran, the 1986 US bombing of Libya, and Operation Desert Storm in 1991 when they joined temporarily based B-52 bombers for bombing missions.

The UK served as a critical hub for communications and intelligence sharing between the United States and other NATO countries during the Cold War. British military and

Left: An aerial view of a portion of the base. The 81st Tactical Fighter Wing, US Air Force Europe (USAFE), at Bentwaters. (Combined Military Service Digital Photographic Files)

Below: Exterior image of the recently completed dependent's newly completed school at the joint British US airbase.

intelligence agencies cooperated closely with their American counterparts, exchanging information, conducting joint operations, and coordinating defence strategies.

As part of the NATO alliance, the US also stationed nuclear weapons on UK soil as a deterrent against potential Soviet aggression. US nuclear weapons were stored at various RAF bases in the UK, including RAF Greenham Common and RAF Upper Heyford.

The story of US operations on UK soil is told at Bentwaters Cold War Museum, on tours at Upper Heyford and at a number of air museums, including RAF Museum Midlands, the American Air Museum at IWM Duxford, the Yorkshire Air Museum and the National Museum of Flight. Local communities fondly recall the communities that grew up around these airbases and that created many jobs. Several US airbases hosted open days for local communities.

A Ground Launch Cruise Missile Launch Control Centre arrives at Greenham Common aboard a C-5 Galaxy.

Mirage F1 at a 1986 open day at Greenham Common.

F-111 flown by the 20th Tactical Fighter Wing, 3rd Air Force, RAF Upper Heyford.

Examples of currently operational US airbases in the UK include RAF Lakenheath and RAF Mildenhall, both of which offer viewing areas for visitors.

The RAF Alconbury bunker, operational from 1989 to 1991, was specifically constructed to service and maintain avionics components installed in the TR-1 aircraft during that era. Contrary to previous assumptions, the building was not named 'Magic Mountain' by base personnel but 'Dragon Mountain'. This moniker aligns with the nomenclature of TR-1 aircraft at Alconbury, known as 'Dragon Lady', and the self-designation of 17 TRW personnel as 'Dragon Keepers'.

Above: RAF Alconbury from the air.

Left: Lockheed TR1A spy plane base at USAAF Alconbury.

Analysing TR1A data in the 'Drgaon Mountain' – a biological and chemical warfare bunker nuclear resilience at RAF Alconbury.

The entrance to Dragon Mountain.

Following the end of the Cold War in 1991, the United States Strategic Command replaced SAC on 1 June 1992. However, the US military presence in the UK continued, albeit decreasing over time. In 2015, plans were announced for the closure of RAF Alconbury and RAF Molesworth by 2020, while RAF Mildenhall was initially scheduled for closure in 2023 but was later postponed indefinitely in 2020. RAF Lakenheath remained an important base, with the deployment of USAF Lockheed Martin F-35 Lightning II aircraft beginning in 2017 and plans for permanent basing from 2021.

16

COMMUNICATIONS TECHNOLOGY

During the Cold War, various communication technologies were used and developed to support military operations, intelligence gathering, and diplomatic efforts. The UK invested in developing secure communication networks to protect sensitive information from interception. These networks employed encryption and encryption-breaking techniques, including advanced cypher systems, to ensure secure communication channels for military and intelligence purposes.

In the late 1950s, Royal Signals planners, anticipating the use of computers to support command and control, planned the fielding of an integrated, networked communications system. Various projects were proposed but foundered through lack of funding or difficulties with international cooperation. However, part of the vision was realised with the introduction of the Clansman range of radios in the early 1970s. At the time, these radios were the most advanced in the world, and they are still in service at every level of command throughout the whole army. Visitors can learn more about Clansman at the Royal Signals Museum on Blandford Camp.

Clansman Radio.

An aerial view of a communications site at RAF Chicksands. The 693rd Electronic Security Wing, Electronic Security Command (ESC), the 6950th Electronic Security Group (ESC) and the Department of Defense Joint Operations Center.

AWDREY

AWDREY, short for Atomic Weapons Detection, Recognition, and Estimation of Yield, was a Cold War-era automatic detection instrument developed by AWRE and deployed at twelve of the twenty-five Royal Observer Corps (ROC) control centres across the UK. Its role was to detect nuclear explosions and estimate their megatonnage. Housed in a 3-foot steel cabinet, AWDREY used photosensitive cells to record the characteristic double flash of light produced by a nuclear blast. The time gap between these flashes allowed for yield estimation and directional indication, with a range of 150 miles. AWDREY was supplemented with DIADEM, which measured electromagnetic pulses. It was operational from 1968 to 1992 and continuously tested.

The development and expansion of telephone exchange systems were crucial for secure and reliable communication during the Cold War. These systems enabled encrypted voice communications between military and government entities. High-frequency (HF) radio networks were extensively used for long-range communication during the Cold War. These networks provided the means to establish communication links over significant distances, including between military bases and remote locations. The Post Office Tower (now the BT Tower) also played a crucial role in telecommunications during the Cold War. It served as a communications hub, hosting antennas for radio, television, and microwave transmissions, which formed the backbone system to ensure effective communications during any potential war.

A map of the 'Backbone' system as conceived in a GPO report in 1956.

JODRELL BANK

Jodrell Bank Observatory near Manchester played a significant role during the Cold War as a key centre for tracking and monitoring space activities, including those related to military and scientific purposes. It was on standby to be part of the Western world's early warning system against potential missile attacks before RAF Fylingdales was completed. Its large radio telescopes had the capability to track and monitor artificial satellites and intercontinental ballistic missiles (ICBMs) launched by both the United States and the Soviet Union. This information was vital for assessing any potential threat to the UK and Western Europe.

The observatory's advanced tracking capabilities were used to monitor the movements and orbits of satellites, both military and civilian. This surveillance was essential for the intelligence community to gather information about Soviet space activities, such as satellite launches and space-based weapon development.

During the Cold War, various arms control agreements were negotiated between the superpowers, including the Strategic Arms Limitation Treaty (SALT). Jodrell Bank played a role in verifying compliance with these agreements by tracking the number and behaviour of satellites and ICBMs, helping to ensure that both sides adhered to their commitments.

Beyond its military applications, Jodrell Bank continued its scientific research into astrophysics and radio astronomy. This research contributed to our understanding of the universe and had implications for both civilian and military technologies. It involved scientists from the UK, the US, and the USSR. The facility remained politically neutral throughout the Cold War period.

The Lovell Telescope at Jodrell Bank.

In preparation for potential conflicts, British telephone lines were classified into three categories: one, two, and three. Category three lines were automatically disconnected in emergencies, category two lines remained connected during peacetime crises, and category one lines were never disconnected. This ensured that if phones stayed connected, it indicated the property's official designation for critical purposes and meant that property owners might soon be visited by officials commandeering the use of a particular property.

Underwater submarine communication cables played a vital role in transmitting secure and encrypted messages between the UK and other countries. These cables facilitated secure and reliable communication between military command centres, intelligence agencies, and government entities. They were laid from a number of locations, but perhaps the most significant were those from Porthcurno, Cornwall, and Harlech in Wales, which both served as the terminus for multiple transatlantic submarine cables, connecting the UK with North America, Felixstowe, which served as a landing site for submarine cables connecting the UK with mainland Europe, and Skewjack, situated near Land's End in Cornwall, which served as a landing site for submarine cables connecting the UK with various destinations, including the Mediterranean region.

The use of satellites for communication purposes expanded during the Cold War. Satellites provided reliable and secure long-distance communication links, enabling the transmission of voice, data, and images across vast distances. They played a crucial role in military command and control, intelligence gathering, and diplomatic communications.

Mobile use of 'single channel' radio access – the military mobile 'phone'. Investment by the Ministry of Defence in new technology for Ptarmigan had a significant impact on the civilian telecommunications world. Ptarmigan's switching technology provided a basis for the modern BT network, and its approach to mobile communications influenced the development of the mobile phone. Visitors can learn more about the revolutionary technology behind Ptarmigan at the Royal Signals Museum on Blandford Camp.

Porthcurno. The clifftop pyramid was constructed after the demolition of the Porthcurno to Brest (France) submarine telegraph cable termination hut at Porthcurno. (Chris Angove)

Ptarmigan radio system.

Traditional radio communication and Morse code also continued to be used during the Cold War, particularly in military contexts. These methods allowed for reliable and relatively secure communication over long distances, often using coded messages to protect sensitive information.

The development and refinement of cryptographic systems was of paramount importance during the Cold War. Both sides of the Cold War invested heavily in cryptography to protect their own communications while also attempting to break the codes and cyphers used by their adversaries. This led to significant advancements in encryption algorithms and codebreaking techniques. This competition spurred advancements in various fields, including telecommunications, encryption, and information processing, that have had a lasting impact on communication technology to this day.

The Cold War era witnessed the rapid advancement of computer technology, which played a crucial role in communication and information processing. Computers were used for data encryption, decryption, and communication network management. The development of computer networks such as ARPANET (the precursor to the internet) also laid the foundation for modern global communication systems.

17

THE COLD WAR IN POPULAR CULTURE

The Cold War had a significant impact on various forms of artistic expression, reflecting the tensions, fears, and ideologies of the era. Artists explored themes related to the Cold War through paintings, sculptures, and installations. They depicted images of nuclear bombs, military conflicts, divided cities, and ideological struggles. Art often conveyed a sense of unease, political critique, and the human cost of the Cold War.

Cold War themes were prevalent in literature, particularly in spy novels and dystopian fiction. Writers like George Orwell (*Nineteen Eighty-Four*) and John le Carré (*The Spy Who Came in from the Cold*) depicted the atmosphere of surveillance, espionage, and political intrigue during the era. These works reflected the psychological and moral dilemmas of individuals caught in the ideological divide.

The Cold War also served as a backdrop for many films, particularly in the genres of spy thrillers and science fiction. Movies like *Dr Strangelove* (1964), *The Day After* (1983), and *WarGames* (1983) explored the nuclear threat, political tensions, and the potential consequences of a global conflict. These films often provided social commentary on the fears and anxieties of the time. The BBC production *Threads* (1984) offered a dramatic account of nuclear war and its effects on the city of Sheffield.

Music also played a significant role in expressing the sentiments of the Cold War. Protest songs and folk music, in particular, conveyed messages of peace, anti-war sentiments, and opposition to nuclear weapons. Artists like Bob Dylan, Joan Baez, and Pete Seeger used their music to raise awareness about the Cold War and advocate for social change. Many songs from the era reflected the fears, tensions, and political climate of the Cold War:

- 'We Didn't Start the Fire' by Billy Joel (1989): A rapid-fire chronicle of historical events, including references to the Berlin Wall, the arms race, and the Cuban Missile Crisis. It highlights the impact of the Cold War on global events and the fear of nuclear conflict.
- '99 Luftballons' by Nena (1983): Originally recorded in German and later released in English as '99 Red Balloons', this song tells the story of ninety-nine balloons being mistaken for an incoming missile attack, leading to escalating tensions and the outbreak of war. It reflects the paranoia and fear of accidental nuclear war during the Cold War era.
- 'The Man Who Sold the World' by David Bowie (1970): While not explicitly about the Cold War, this song has been interpreted as referencing the Cold War and the threat of nuclear destruction. It conveys a sense of alienation and uncertainty prevalent during the era.

- 'Russians' by Sting (1985): This song reflects on the Cold War from a perspective of hope and understanding. Sting sings about the shared humanity between Russians and Westerners, urging for peace and nuclear disarmament.
- 'Eve of Destruction' by Barry McGuire (1965): Although released during the early stages of the Cold War, this song captured the anxiety and fear surrounding the conflict. It expressed concerns about the potential devastation caused by nuclear weapons and the implications of the Cold War for humanity.
- 'Radio Free Europe' by R.E.M. (1981): This song alludes to the Radio Free Europe broadcasts during the Cold War, which aimed to counter communist propaganda. It reflects a sense of defiance and the struggle for freedom of information.
- 'Two Tribes' by Frankie Goes to Hollywood (1984): This song depicts the tensions between the United States and the Soviet Union during the Cold War. It uses the metaphor of a boxing match to symbolise the potential for nuclear war and the need for a peaceful resolution.
- 'Land of Confusion' by Genesis (1986): While not explicitly about the Cold War, this song's music video features puppets of world leaders, including Ronald Reagan and Mikhail Gorbachev. The imagery reflects the nuclear arms race and the political climate of the time.
- 'Back in the USSR' by The Beatles (1968): This song takes a light-hearted approach, referencing the Cold War through its lyrics about a fictional trip to the Soviet Union. It juxtaposes the tension of the era with a catchy, upbeat melody.
- 'The War Song' by Culture Club (1984): This song addresses the threat of nuclear war and the need for peace. It emphasises unity and advocates against violence, reflecting the fears and concerns of the Cold War era.

Some performance artists used their medium to challenge the ideologies and systems associated with the Cold War. Their works often addressed political censorship, propaganda, and the impact of militarism. Performance art provided a platform for artists to question societal norms and express dissent. Cold War themes were also sometimes represented in street art and graffiti, particularly in locations close to military installations or areas with political significance. Artists used murals, stencils, and other forms of street art to convey political messages, challenge authority, and provoke dialogue.

The fall of the Berlin Wall and the breakup of the USSR also led to a number of pop-culture hits, including 'Wind of Change' by the Scorpions (1991), which became an anthem of hope and freedom associated with the fall of the Berlin Wall and reunification of Germany, while songs such as Heroes by David Bowie (1977) gained renewed significance during the fall of the Berlin Wall, with its lyrics reflecting the spirit of defiance and unity.

Interestingly, the fascination with post-apocalyptic life continued in the post-Cold War period. The genre continues to captivate audiences with its exploration of a world transformed by cataclysmic events and the human struggle to adapt and endure. Popular examples include *Blast From the Past* (1999), *28 Days Later* (2002), *I Am Legend* (2007), *The Road* (2009), *The Book of Eli* (2010), *Mad Max: Fury Road* (2015), and *10 Cloverfield Lane* (2016).

A crowd of West German citizens gathers at the newly created opening in the Berlin Wall at Potsdamer Platz. (Combined Military Service Digital Photographic Files)

18

THE CAMPAIGN FOR NUCLEAR DISARMAMENT

The Campaign for Nuclear Disarmament (CND) was founded in the United Kingdom in 1958 at a time when the Cold War tensions between the United States and the Soviet Union were escalating, leading to an arms race and the development of nuclear weapons. The organisation emerged in response to public concern about the devastating consequences of nuclear weapons and the potential for global annihilation. It advocates for disarmament, non-proliferation, and the redirection of resources from nuclear weapons programmes towards social welfare, healthcare, education, and other humanitarian needs.

CND is known for its active involvement in organising protests, demonstrations, and other forms of direct action to raise public awareness about the dangers of nuclear weapons. The organisation has arranged large-scale marches, rallies, and sit-ins, including the famous Aldermaston Marches held in the late 1950s and early 1960s. CND has also campaigned against the deployment of nuclear weapons in various locations, such as military bases and missile sites.

In the early 1980s, the United States deployed Ground-Launched Cruise Missiles (GLCMs) at Greenham Common as part of NATO's response to the perceived threat of Soviet nuclear weapons. This deployment sparked widespread public opposition and protests due to concerns about nuclear proliferation and the potential for nuclear war.

CND march in Caernarfon on 22 March 1962.

Cruise missile base at Greenham Common. (Combined Military Service Digital Photographic Files)

An aerial view of the ground-launched cruise missile base at Royal Air Force Molesworth, home to the 303rd Tactical Missile Wing. (Combined Military Service Digital Photographic Files)

THE WOMEN'S PEACE CAMP

In September 1981, a group of women organised a peace camp near the perimeter fence of the Greenham Common RAF base. Their objective was to protest against the presence of nuclear weapons and call for their removal. The protest became known as the Greenham Common Women's Peace Camp and soon gained international attention. The women at the peace camp engaged in various forms of direct action to disrupt operations and draw attention to their cause.

Anti-nuclear demonstrators camped outside the airbase during the arrival of the Ground Launch Cruise Missile equipment. (Combined Military Service Digital Photographic Files)

These actions included cutting through fences, blocking roads, and interfering with the movement of military vehicles. They aimed to challenge the militarisation of the base and raise awareness about the dangers of nuclear weapons. The women at Greenham Common used symbolic actions to convey their anti-nuclear message. One notable example was the establishment of the 'Embrace the Base' campaign in December 1982, during which thousands of women formed a human chain around the base's perimeter fence. They sought to emphasise the need for peace and disarmament.

The Greenham Common Women's Peace Camp remained active for almost two decades, with women continuously living at the camp and engaging in non-violent protest activities. The movement inspired similar peace camps and protests in other parts of the world.

The protests at Greenham Common and the activism of the women's peace camp had a lasting impact. They contributed to a wider public debate on nuclear disarmament, influenced political discourse, and raised awareness about the potential consequences of nuclear weapons. The protests also played a role in shaping public opinion and contributed to the eventual removal of the missiles from Greenham Common in 1991.

The protests at Greenham Common exemplified the power of grassroots activism and the significant role that CND and other peace movements played in raising awareness about nuclear disarmament during the Cold War.

While the Campaign for Nuclear Disarmament is based in the UK, it has had an impact beyond its borders. CND has collaborated with similar organisations around the world and participated in international peace and disarmament movements. It has been involved in discussions at the United Nations and has contributed to the global discourse on nuclear disarmament. It has played a significant role in shaping public opinion and influencing political discourse on nuclear disarmament. It has raised awareness about the humanitarian and environmental consequences of nuclear weapons and has contributed to the signing of international treaties and agreements, such as the Treaty on the Non-Proliferation of Nuclear Weapons (NPT). CND continues to advocate for disarmament and peace through its campaigns, lobbying efforts, and educational activities.

CND march in Aberystwyth, May 1961.

19

PROTECT AND SURVIVE

'Protect and Survive' was a public information series created by the British government during the 1970s and 1980s, specifically during the height of Cold War tensions between the West and the Soviet Union. The purpose of 'Protect and Survive' was to inform and educate the public on how to protect themselves and survive in the event of a nuclear attack. It is the only real information about the period that was in the public domain, beyond news accounts of specific crises of the period.

It covered a range of topics, including preparing and reinforcing homes, constructing shelters, managing food and water supplies, and dealing with potential fallout and radiation. The information was released as a series of booklets and public information films. The booklets provided detailed instructions and illustrations, while the films demonstrated various survival techniques and procedures.

Protect and survive booklet.
(Crown Copyright)

Guidance for preparing a fallout shelter at home. (Crown Copyright)

The information generated significant controversy and debate. Critics argued that the advice provided was inadequate and that survival in a nuclear war would be highly unlikely. Some saw the campaign as an attempt to shift responsibility onto the individual rather than focusing on disarmament and peace efforts. As a consequence, the public response to 'Protect and Survive' varied.

Some people took the information seriously and made efforts to prepare for potential nuclear attacks, while others dismissed it as unrealistic or fearmongering. The campaign's impact on public perception of nuclear war and civil defence remains a topic of discussion.

With the easing of Cold War tensions and the improved relations between the West and the Soviet Union, public interest in civil defence and the 'Protect and Survive' campaign waned. The campaign became less relevant, and the materials were eventually discontinued.

20

RAISING THE ALARM

In the 1950s and 1960s, the General Post Office (GPO) held a monopoly on landline and licensed wireless communications in the UK. Over time, the Post Office's telecommunications branch evolved into British Telecom (BT), becoming a private company and losing its monopoly status.

One of the notable services introduced by the GPO was the Speaking Clock in 1936, which quickly became popular across the UK. To ensure its uninterrupted operation, a redundant system of communication was established between major telephone exchanges, designed to raise alarms in case of failures. This redundancy helped maintain the reliability of the Speaking Clock or Time Signal (TIM) service.

During the Cold War, the need arose for a national communications system to relay attack warnings from command centres to 250 control points in police stations across the country. The existing Speaking Clock distribution system, known for its reliability, was repurposed to distribute vital national warning messages.

The attack warning information was derived from military radar and the US Ballistic Missile Early Warning System. The UK Warning and Monitoring Organisation (UKWMO) took responsibility for fallout warnings and the eventual all-clear messages. Each of the twenty-five UKWMO group controls was connected by landline to police station control points within its coverage area.

While Second World War air-raid sirens remained available for use in urban areas to then sound public alarms, those living in rural communities relied on simpler solutions. Speech receivers were strategically placed within establishments like post offices, shops, pubs, vicarages, or the residences of trusted figures such as police officers, council officials, or magistrates. These individuals were considered 'responsible' and relied upon hand sirens, whistles, maroons, and gongs to alert the local community. Approximately 18,000 warning points were distributed across the country.

To broadcast messages and control sirens, police station control points utilised a carrier signal sent over normal telephone circuits. This system, known as the Carrier Control Point (CCP), was highly effective, didn't disrupt telephone lines, and was cost-effective compared to the Private Wire system used during the Second World War.

The initial HANDEL (the code-name for the UK's national attack warning system) and carrier networks were installed in the early 1960s and were upgraded to a second generation in the 1980s. These systems served until the end of the Cold War in 1992. Following a review of emergency planning in 1991, the Royal Observer Corps (R.O.C.) was stood down, and in 1992, the UKWMO ceased operations. Consequently, HANDEL and the carrier broadcast system were decommissioned.

The equipment, originally managed by the GPO and later by British Telecom, saw advancements like the replacement of mechanical speaking clocks with electronic units in 1984. Even after HANDEL's closure, the electronic clocks and analogue distribution network continued to operate in the UK until 1994, when they were replaced by digital Recorded Information Distribution Equipment (RIDE). These digital systems marked the end of the HANDEL era and improved information distribution efficiency.

21

THE WARTIME BROADCASTING SERVICE

Internally, the BBC referred to the Wartime Broadcasting Service (WTBS) as the 'Deferred Facility' or simply 'DF', a distinction from the abbreviation for radio Direction Finding. The pre-attack national programme would originate from an underground bunker at the BBC Training School, Wood Norton, located 2.5 miles north-west of Evesham, Worcestershire. Regional Government Headquarters (RGHQ) were also all equipped with basic studios, enabling regions to deviate from the national programme source to convey locally relevant information.

In the 1970s, there was limited fallout protection and standby power. By the 1980s, efforts were made to provide fallout-protected accommodations for staff at various locations, including Moorside Edge, Stagshaw, Burghead, Black Hill, Start Point, Brookmans Park, Washford, Sutton Coldfield, and Wenvoe. Additionally, existing protected accommodations at Droitwich, Wrotham, Westerglen, Lisnagarvey, Holme Moss, Oxford, North Hessary Tor, Daventry, and Clevedon were refurbished.

Moorside Edge transmitter building, now the medium wave transmitter for BBC Radio 5 in the north. (MarkT, CC BY-SA 2.0)

Wood Norton Hall before the BBC arrived. Used during the Second World War as a station for listening to enemy radio broadcasts and an emergency broadcasting centre, it became the accommodation for the BBC's engineering training college that grew up on its grounds. The BBC retained purpose-built facilities in the grounds for technical training after selling the hall, which is now a hotel.

Essential transmitters at Black Hill, Droitwich, and Start Point, lacking standby generators, were slated to receive them to ensure WTBS operation in the likely event of a disruption in the normal electricity supply. Furthermore, WTBS studios at Wood Norton were set to undergo upgrades, including the installation of an EMP screen, improved air conditioning, replacement diesel generators, and the establishment of a new standby WTBS studio at an undisclosed location, all slated for completion by 1988–89. Many of these works remained incomplete as Cold War provisions were disbanded.

BBC Transcript to Be Used in Wake of Nuclear Attack

This is the Wartime Broadcasting Service.

This country has been attacked with nuclear weapons. Communications have been severely disrupted, and the number of casualties and the extent of the damage are not yet known. We shall bring you further information as soon as possible. Meanwhile, stay tuned to this wavelength, stay calm and stay in your own homes. Remember, there is nothing to be gained by trying to get away. By leaving your homes, you could be exposing yourselves to greater danger. If you leave, you may find yourself without food, without water, without accommodation and without protection.

Radioactive fall-out, which follows a nuclear explosion, is many times more dangerous if you are directly exposed to it in the open. Roofs and walls offer substantial protection. The safest place is indoors. Make sure gas and other fuel supplies are turned off and that all fires are extinguished. If mains water is available, this can be used for fire-fighting. You should also refill all your containers for drinking water after the fires have been put out because the main water supply may not be available for very long. Water must not be used for flushing lavatories: until you are told that lavatories may be used again, other toilet arrangements must be made. Use your water only for essential drinking and cooking purposes. Water means life. Don't waste it. Make your food stocks last: ration your supply because it may have to last for 14 days or more. If you have fresh food in the house, use this first to avoid wasting it: food in tins will keep. If you live in an area where a fall-out warning has been given, stay in your fall-out room until you are told it is safe to come out. When the immediate danger has passed, the sirens will sound a steady note.

The 'all clear' message will also be given on this wavelength. If you leave the fall-out room to go to the lavatory or replenish food or water supplies, do not remain outside the room for a minute longer than is necessary. Do not, in any circumstances, go outside the house. Radioactive fall-out can kill. You cannot see it or feel it, but it is there. If you go outside, you will bring danger to your family, and you may die. Stay in your fall-out room until you are told it is safe to come out, or you hear the 'all clear' on the sirens. Here are the main points again:

- Stay in your own homes, and if you live in an area where a fall-out warning has been given, stay in your fall-out room until you are told it is safe to come out.
- The message that the immediate danger has passed will be given by the sirens and repeated on this wavelength.
- Make sure that the gas and all fuel supplies are turned off and that all fires are extinguished.
- Water must be rationed and used only for essential drinking and cooking purposes.
- It must not be used for flushing lavatories.
- Ration your food supply: it may have to last for 14 days or more. We shall repeat this broadcast in two hours' time.

Stay tuned to this wavelength, but switch your radios off now to save your batteries until we come on the air again. That is the end of this broadcast.

22

BRITAIN'S NUCLEAR DETERRENT

Since the end of the V-Force era, Britain's nuclear deterrent has been maintained through the Trident system. Trident is a submarine-launched ballistic missile (SLBM) system that consists of nuclear-powered submarines armed with Trident II D5 missiles. The submarines are part of the Royal Navy's Vanguard-class, which currently consists of four submarines: HMS *Vanguard*, HMS *Victorious*, HMS *Vigilant*, and HMS *Vengeance*.

Britain's nuclear deterrent is maintained through a policy of continuous at-sea deterrence (CASD). This means that at least one Trident submarine is on patrol at all times,

Polaris nuclear missile fired from submarine – Polaris missiles were used by the UK between 1968 and 1996. Each of the UK's four Resolution-class submarines was armed with sixteen Polaris A3 missiles.

ensuring that a credible nuclear deterrent is available and ready for use. The Trident II D5 missiles carried by the Vanguard-class submarines have a range that allows them to strike targets at intercontinental distances. These missiles are equipped with multiple independently targetable re-entry vehicles (MIRVs), which means that each missile can carry multiple warheads capable of targeting separate locations.

The UK's possession of nuclear weapons and its operation of the Trident system provide it with an independent nuclear deterrent. Unlike some other countries, the UK maintains full operational control over its nuclear weapons and does not rely on assistance or cooperation from other nations.

Above: Vickers Armstrong at Barrow-in-Furness constructing a nuclear submarine.

Right: BAE systems at Barrow-in-Furness.

GAZETTEER

The information contained in this gazetteer was correct at the time of publication. We chose not to include websites as many projects are under development and details may change. Please contact each individual attraction before visiting to make sure that details are correct and access is possible. Please note that postcodes may be close to the specific site and do not indicate access or viewing is possible.

South West

Aerospace Bristol
Bristol, BS34 5BZ
Aerospace Bristol tells the incredible story of Bristol's amazing aviation achievements and gives you and your family the chance to step aboard Concorde Alpha Foxtrot, the last of the supersonic jets ever to fly. There is loads to discover at Aerospace Bristol, starting from the earliest days of powered flight through to today's cutting-edge aerospace technology.

Berry Head Fort and Battery and Hardy's Head Battery
Brixham, Devon, TQ5 9AP
Berry Head is a National Nature Reserve. This stunning headland, with its iconic lighthouse and Napoleonic Fort, is surrounded by water on three sides and offers exceptional views across Torbay and beyond. It includes the remains of military buildings dating back to the Napoleonic period. Part of the store building was reused as a Royal Observer Corps post, and in 1960 an underground monitoring post was built within what appears to have been a cistern within the store building.

Davidstow Moor RAF Museum
Camelford, Cornwall, PL32 9YF
The museum is housed in the former Sergeants Shower Block and offers the visitor a remarkable insight into the history of the former RAF airfield. The museum has many artefacts and a wealth of personal memories from those who flew and worked at Davidstow Moor.

Farnborough Air Sciences Trust Museum
Farnborough, Hampshire, GU14 6TF
Farnborough Air Sciences Trust (FAST) exists to safeguard and promote Farnborough's great heritage in aviation science. The FAST Museum adjacent to Farnborough Airfield

holds a collection of aircraft (actual and model), satellites, simulators and other unique materials related to Farnborough's world-famous Royal Aircraft Establishment. FAST also offers exclusive guided tours of areas of Farnborough's historic aviation quarter that are not normally open to the public.

Goonhilly Downs
Helston, Cornwall, TR12 6LQ
Located in the most southerly peninsula in England, this conservation area and its numerous coves provide a rich range of natural habitats that will reward birdwatchers and naturalists. Walks around the area offer views of the Goonhilly Satellite Earth Station.

Fleet Air Arm Museum
Ilchester, Somerset, BA22 8HT
The Fleet Air Arm Museum is devoted to the history of British naval aviation. It has an extensive collection of military and civilian aircraft, aero engines, models of aircraft and Royal Navy ships, and paintings and drawings related to naval aviation.

The Helicopter Museum
Weston-super-Mare, Somerset, BS24 8PP
The award-winning Helicopter Museum holds over 100 Rotary wing aircraft gathered from all over the world, representing a wide spectrum of technologies. Visitor favourites include two of the Queen's Royal Flight helicopters, the current world speed record holder G-LYNX (400 km per hour), a Vietnam Veteran Huey, a Russian Hind Gun Ship, and much more.

Nothe Fort
Weymouth, Dorset, DT4 8UF
In 1970, the military no longer needed the fort. Weymouth Civic Society volunteers began restoration, and the Nothe Fort Museum of Coastal Defence opened to the public. In 1980, the council converted part of the underground magazine area into an emergency Civil Defence Nuclear Bunker. This was decommissioned in 1990 after the collapse of the Soviet Union. Today, visitors can explore the maze of underground tunnels, visit the Victorian Gun Deck, sit on the impressive Second Word War gun high up on the ramparts, discover the secret underground nuclear bunker or simply enjoy stunning 360-degree views of Dorset's Jurassic Coast.

RAF Portland
Portland, Dorset, DT5 1FR
Royal Air Force Portland, or more simply RAF Portland, is a former Royal Air Force and ROTOR radar station on the Isle of Portland, Dorset, England. Located close to the Verne Citadel and East Cliff, the station was established in the 1950s as part of a nationwide air defence radar system built by the British Government during the Cold War. The station became a scheduled monument in 2004 and is now the site of the community farm, Fancy's Family Farm.

Royal Electrical and Mechanical Engineers Museum
Lyneham, Chippenham, SN15 4XX
The REME Museum cares for just over 130,000 items. The collections are a fascinating and eclectic mix that focuses on the REME story but also tells us much about the British Army in the twentieth and twenty-first centuries.

Royal Signals Museum
Blandford Camp, Dorset, DT11 8RH
Situated on Blandford Camp in Dorset, the Royal Signals Museum preserves and promotes the history of the Royal Corps of Signals via interactive displays and stories from its oral history library, highlighting the Corps' communications role within BAOR (British Army of the Rhine), the museum charts the technological shift from BRUIN to Ptarmigan. It explores how global Cold War taskings were responsible for groundbreaking innovations in electronic warfare and signals intelligence. Closer to home, vehicles and equipment help explain how the Corps would have provided communications to regional governments in preparation for a nuclear strike. Plan your visit: www.royalsignalsmuseum.co.uk.

The Tank Museum
Bovington, Dorset, BH20 6JG
The Tank Museum brings history to life with the world's best collection of tanks and explosive live displays. Come face to face with over 300 huge military machines and hear about amazing experiences as you explore nine powerful and awe-inspiring exhibitions covering over a century of history.

SOUTH

Brooklands Museum
Weybridge, Surrey, KT13 0SL
Brooklands Museum is on the site of the world's first purpose-built motor racing circuit. After the war, the race circuit was in poor condition as trees had been planted into the concrete to help screen the Hawker and Vickers aircraft factories. The site was sold to Vickers-Armstrong in 1946 for continued use as an aircraft factory. The Valiant V bomber was built here.

Gatwick Aviation Museum
Gatwick, Surrey, RH6 0BT
Founded in 1987, Gatwick Aviation Museum began as a private collection acquired by local Surrey businessman Peter Vallance. The collection includes Cold War-era jets.

Greenham Control Tower
Newbury, Berkshire, RG19 8BZ
The former Control Tower dates from 1951–53 with 1980s modifications. Greenham Control Tower was opened to the public in 2018. Views from the upper observation deck look out 360 degrees across the common and the old runaway, with good views of the bunkers built to house ninety-six missiles. A permanent exhibition focuses on the history of the building and the stories of those who were connected with it whilst it was operational.

Greenham Common Control Tower.

Kennedy Memorial Landscape
Runnymede, Surrey, TW20 0AE
A memorial garden for President John F. Kennedy. The acre of land on which it is set, a gift to America, overlooks the valley in which the Magna Carta was signed.

The Museum of Military Medicine
Aldershot, Hampshire, GU12 5RQ
The museum tells the story of army medicine and healthcare, human and animal, from the English Civil War to the current day.

Needles Battery
Alum Bay, Isle of Wight, PO39 0JH
The New Battery is set between the Needles Old Battery and Tennyson Down. It was built in 1895 after concerns were raised about the firing of the guns at the Old Battery, causing the cliffs to crumble. This battery was used throughout the First and Second World War. Then, once decommissioned, the fortified underground rooms were ideal for housing the nerve centre of a highly secret operation to test rockets here between the 1950s and 1970s. This area tells the fascinating story of British-made space rockets Black Knight and Black Arrow. You can stand at the site of the testing gantries and see where the sounds and smells of early rocket technology used the isolated site and sea beyond to shield its secrets.

The Royal Gunpowder Mills
Waltham Abbey, Hertfordshire, EN9 1JY
300 years of intrigue and history in a stunning natural setting are ready to explore. Visitor activities, busy school programmes, talks, walks, tractor tours, railway rides, exhibitions, workshops and re-enactments are among the ways visitors can explore and enjoy this unique site this year. Much of the 170-acre site is now a scheduled ancient monument and Site of Special Scientific Interest.

The Royal Navy Submarine Museum
Gosport, Hampshire, PO12 2AS
Take a deep dive into the fascinating world of submarines at the Royal Navy Submarine Museum. As well as HMS *Alliance*, the only remaining Second World War submarine,

visitors can explore other submarines as well as photographs, documents, ship plans, and artefacts. Displays include a look into the personal accounts of those serving onboard Britain's at-sea nuclear deterrent programme at the Silent and Secret Gallery.

Greater London

HMS *Belfast*
The Queen's Walk, London, SE1 2JH
HMS *Belfast* was launched on St Patrick's Day, 17 March, 1938 and saw active service during the Second World War and the Korean War. Its final years were spent performing peace-keeping duties until she retired from service in 1963.

Imperial War Museum
Lambeth Road, London, SE1 6HZ
IWM London is the world's leading museum of war. Founded during the First World War, it gives voice to the extraordinary experiences of ordinary people forced to live their lives in a world torn apart by conflict. Displayed across six floors, the museum's vast collections encompass a wealth of objects.

National Army Museum
Royal Hospital Road, London, SW3 4HT
The National Army Museum's five dynamic galleries show thousands of objects from across the collections. They tell a huge range of stories from the army's history. The galleries offer many perspectives, addressing fundamental questions such as 'Why do we have an army?', examining the army's relationship with society, and showing how it has touched virtually every part of the world.

RAF Museum London
Grahame Park Way, London, NW9 5LL
Explore spacious indoor hangars and enjoy learning about flying machines with your kids. Meet the RAF and its unique people, take part in an RAF mission and learn about the brave RAF men and women. The whole family will be able to enjoy the interactive exhibitions exploring the first 100 years of the RAF.

Royal Arsenal Woolwich
Artillery Square, Woolwich, London, SE18 4DX
The former site of one of the biggest ammunition factories in the UK, the Royal Arsenal has been regenerated as an open space and place to live and will be further transformed by development.

The Science Museum
Exhibition Road, South Kensington, London, SW7 2DD
The Science Museum is part of the Science Museum Group, the world's leading group of science museums that share a world-class collection providing an enduring record of scientific, technological and medical achievements from across the globe. Over the last century, the Science Museum, the home of human ingenuity, has grown in scale and scope,

The Science Museum. (© Science Museum Group)

inspiring visitors with exhibitions covering topics as diverse as robots, code-breaking, cosmonauts and superbugs. The Science Museum was named a winner of the prestigious Art Fund Museum of the Year prize for 2020.

South East

Chartwell
Westerham, Kent, TN16 1PS

At the end of the Second World War, with the Allies victorious, Winston Churchill was part of the critical decision-making that shaped global politics in the twentieth century. Present at Yalta and briefly the Potsdam conference, Churchill was involved in major Cold War events through until his death in 1965. At Westminster College in Fulton, Missouri, he gave his era-defining 'Iron Curtain' speech that would shape the relationship between West and East. Chartwell in Kent became his home in 1922 and hosted several important visits, including one by the former US President Harry Truman.

Chatham Historic Dockyard
Chatham, Kent, ME4 4TZ

A visit to the Historic Dockyard Chatham, one of Britain's leading maritime heritage destinations, is a guaranteed adventure. The site includes a Second World War warship, the National Collection of Historic Lifeboats, and a former Cold War submarine. Chatham was producing submarines until 1966, well into the Cold War period.

Cuckfield ROC Post
Haywards Heath, West Sussex, RH17 5JZ

First used in 1925 and operated during the Second World War, the bunker was operational during the Cold War and was restored in 2009. It is now open for a limited number of days each year.

Dover Castle
Dover, Kent, CT16 1HU

In the early 1960s, one of twelve regional seats of government (RSG) was installed in a pre-existing tunnel complex on the cliff beneath Dover Castle. The heart of this was in the

Entrance to the tunnels at Dover Castle. (© English Heritage)

lowest level (Dumpy), with parts of the upper two levels refitted as a dormitory, dining and catering areas, and restrooms. The complex continued to expand and evolve in line with changes to Civil Defence planning, including the creation of a small TV broadcasting studio, until the 1980s when it was put on 'care and maintenance' and custodianship was transferred to English Heritage. Today, Dumpy can be visited for occasional specialist tours.

Gravesend Cold War Bunker
Gravesend, Kent, DA13 9HS

This earth- and turf-covered underground structure was built for the local coordination of civil defence responses to an air attack, whether conventional or nuclear. Its thirteen rooms are divided into communications, control rooms for directing operations outside, dormitories and toilets and an emergency power plant. The bunker has been restored to its original appearance. Owned by Gravesham Borough Council, it is opened for guided tours by Thames Defence Heritage.

Gravesend Cold War Bunker.

The Royal Engineers Museum
Gillingham, Kent, ME7 1UR
Visit Kent's largest military museum to discover the story of the Royal Engineers and how they have helped the British Army live, move and fight for over 300 years. With highlights including twenty-five Victoria Crosses, Wellington's map of Waterloo, Chard's weapons from the Zulu War, an amazing collection of bridge-laying tanks, Chinese silks, the world's first guided torpedo, Indian battle axes, a huge piece of the Berlin Wall, Zulu shields, a Harrier Jump Jet and a deadly V2 rocket, it is no surprise that the museum's collection has been designated as being of historical and international importance.

Tangmere Military and Aviation Museum
Chichester, West Sussex, PO20 2ES
In the early 1950s, due to the deteriorating political situation between the West and the Soviet Union, Operational Readiness Platforms (ORPs) were constructed at RAF Tangmere to enable Meteor fighter aircraft (replaced in 1955 with Hunter aircraft) to be held at the end of the runway to facilitate quick reaction. In 1958, it was considered that the threat to the UK would be from across the North Sea, and RAF Tangmere was closed and reopened as the RAF Language to train military personnel as Russian translators. The museum has eight Cold War aircraft in its collection.

Midlands

Broadway Tower ROC Post
Broadway, Worcestershire, WR12 7LB
Our former monitoring bunker was once part of a wider network of similar structures all over the United Kingdom, built to study and report the effects of nuclear explosions and the resulting radioactive fallout.

The Centre for Computing History
Cambridge, CB1 3EW
The Centre for Computing History (CCH) is a pioneering educational charity that opened at its current site in Cambridge in August 2013. CCH was established to tell the story of the Information Age by exploring the historical, social and cultural impact of developments in personal computing.

Drakelow Tunnels
Kidderminster, Shropshire, DY11 5SW
Drakelow Tunnels is a former Second World War underground shadow factory that manufactured aircraft components on behalf of the British aeroplane company. Part of the 3.5-mile tunnel complex was upgraded in the 1960s and designated as a regional seat of government and later a regional government headquarters in the 1980s. When the Cold War ended, the site was sold and later converted into a secure fine wine storage facility. Part of the site has been kept as a museum and is open to the public on a number of days throughout the year.

Entrance to Drakelow Tunnels.

East Midlands Airport Aeropark
Castle Donington, Derbyshire, DE74 2PR
The Aeropark is both an aviation museum and a viewing area where you can study the preserved planes of yesteryear, including several Cold War jets, as well as watching the modern airliners take off and land at a growing international passenger and cargo airport.

Hack Green Nuclear Bunker
Nantwich, Cheshire, CW5 8BL
Hidden deep in the Cheshire countryside, the bunker stayed secret for more than fifty years. Now, the blast doors are open, and you can discover the labyrinth of rooms and authentic equipment used to run this defence region in the event of a national emergency.

Harrington Museum
Harrington, Northampton, NN6 9PF
The Carpetbagger Aviation Museum is housed in the Group Operations Building on the Administration Site of the former Station 179 airfield at Harrington, Northamptonshire. Exhibits and displays include the secret work of the British Special Operations Executive from their RAF base at Tempsford, the Cold War roles of the airfield at Harrington with Thor rockets, and the Royal Observer Corps.

Holbeach ROC Post
Spalding, Lincolnshire, PE12 7PP
Holbeach ROC Monitoring Post was established in 1955 and refitted in 1964 to monitor for nuclear attacks and carry out important observations of the fallout of a nuclear

Holbeach ROC post.

attack happened. Once reopened in 1964, members were trained in identifying an attack, recording the associated fallout and travel of nuclear material, and conveying information back to 15 Group headquarters in Fiskerton, near Lincoln. The site remained active until 1991 when it closed at the culmination of the Cold War. Since 2000, the site has been owned and managed by Heritage Lincolnshire and is accessible for heritage open days and talks.

RAF Holmpton Nuclear Bunker
Holmpton, Hull, HU19 2RG
The former RAF Holmpton is a Cold War nuclear bunker preserved and maintained by a dedicated group of volunteers and veterans. It holds occasional open days.

Jet Age Museum
Meteor Business Park, Gloucester, GL2 9QL
The Jet Age Museum celebrates Gloucestershire's rich aviation heritage from the early days of flight through the birth of the jet age to the present day.

Jodrell Bank
Macclesfield, Cheshire, SK11 9DW
Jodrell Bank is a world-leading deep-space radio observatory, a UNESCO World Heritage Site, and an award-winning national visitor attraction. Explore interactive displays, projections and artefacts as you journey from the early post-war days of Jodrell Bank, through the heights of the space race and the depths of the Cold War, to today's world-leading discoveries.

The Midland Air Museum
Coventry, CV3 4FR
The Midland Air Museum welcomes visitors of all ages to experience the world of aviation in a friendly and informal environment. The Midland Air Museum is a unique aeronautical collection and has something to interest everyone, with over forty-five aircraft on display.

Military Intelligence Museum
JFC, Chicksands, Shefford, Bedfordshire, SG17 5PR
The Military Intelligence Museum tells the story of British military intelligence from the Boer War onwards. We reveal the tactics, techniques and equipment used by the people who have carried out their vitally important tasks across the years, often in secret, with courage and determination, but always without fanfare.

National Radio Centre
Bletchley, Milton Keynes, MK3 6DS
The RSGBs National Radio Centre is a showcase for radio communications technology. It provides the opportunity to find out about the history and development of wireless communication. The timeline spans from the first inventors in the late nineteenth century through to current radio technology, including examples of both the Second World War and Cold War radio equipment. With films, interactive displays and hands-on experiments, there is plenty for visitors to see and even the opportunity to go 'on air' with a modern amateur radio station.

The National Radio Centre.

National Space Centre
Exploration Drive, Leicester, LE4 5NS
The National Space Centre really is a visit that is out of this world. Take a journey through themed galleries, stopping at over 150 interactive experiences! Sit back in awe in the UK's largest planetarium as we take you on a voyage of discovery in this 360° full-dome experience. The National Space Centre is an all-weather attraction for the whole family. On-site, we have over 400 parking spaces, a restaurant, a shop and all the facilities you would expect from a world-class attraction.

The Newark Air Museum
Newark, Nottinghamshire, NG24 2NY
One of the largest volunteer-run aviation museums in the UK, Newark Air Museum is located on the former Second World War airfield of Winthorpe in eastern Nottinghamshire. Its diverse collection of more than ninety aircraft and cockpit sections covers the history of aviation.

National Memorial Arboretum
Burton-on-Trent, Staffordshire, DE13 7AR
Visitors can enjoy discovering over 400 memorials nestled amongst some 25,000 trees, experiencing riverside walks and participating in a wide variety of daily activities, guided walks, land train tours, memorial talks, exhibitions, and buggy tours.

The National Museum of Computing
Bletchley, Milton Keynes, MK3 6EB
Follow the development of computing, from the Turing-Welchman Bombe and Colossus of the 1940s through the large systems and mainframes of the 1950s, 1960s and 1970s to the rise of personal computing and the rise of mobile computing and the internet.

RAF Museum Midlands
Cosford, Shropshire, TF11 8UP
Take off to the RAF Museum Midlands and explore a vast collection of aircraft, vehicles, artefacts, and the fascinating story of the RAF! The museum is home to over seventy-five historic aircraft, including the world's oldest Spitfire, the unique TSR2 and the mighty Vulcan bomber, to name but a few.

Let your imagination take flight inside the National Cold War Exhibition, where you will discover Cold War stories in immersive hotspots. Explore exciting displays of aircraft, iconic cars, tanks, and even a section of the Berlin Wall. Aircraft to be noticed include all three British V-bombers – Vulcan, Victor and Valiant – and the English Electric Lightning suspended vertically.

Sywell Aviation Museum
Sywell Aerodrome, Northampton, NN6 0BN
The Sywell Aviation Museum (SAM) is a voluntary, non-profit organisation which aims to preserve the history of Sywell Aerodrome and Northamptonshire's rich aviation heritage from the early days of aviation to the Second World War and beyond.

East of England

Alconbury Weald

Alconbury, Weald, Huntingdon, PE28 4XA

A new flourishing community, Alconbury Weald is a place to nurture your family, make new friends, grow your business and enjoy seasonal events and entertainment. Alconbury Weald's more recent military history, and particularly its intelligence and reconnaissance role throughout the Second World War and Cold War, is designed into the plans through the layout of parks and squares and design around the Listed Buildings, which commemorate a dynamic history.

Bentwaters Cold War Museum

Woodbridge, Suffolk, IP12 2TW

Bentwaters Cold War Museum is based in the United States Air Force (USAF) hardened command post on the former Bentwaters airbase. The airbase closed after the withdrawal of the USAF in 1993 and is believed to be the only such building open to the public in the UK and Europe. Visitors can experience the Cold War history with guides and talks about the operations of the base with detailed displays of the units stationed at both RAF Bentwaters and nearby RAF Woodbridge since the Second World War.

Chain Home Transmitter Tower at Great Baddow

Chelmsford, Essex, CM2 8HN

Great Baddow Chain Home Tower, erected initially at RAF Canewdon in south-east Essex in 1937, relocated to Great Baddow in 1956, and is the only complete Chain Home transmitter tower surviving in the British Isles, standing to its full height of 109.12 metres (358 feet) and retaining all six working platforms. It can be viewed off Vicarage Lane, Great Baddow, Essex, CM2 8JG.

City of Norwich Aviation Museum

Norwich, NR10 3JF

The City of Norwich Aviation Museum is the home of Norfolk's Aviation Heritage with an outdoor space housing nearly thirty aircraft, cockpit sections and exhibits, which include a Vulcan Bomber and a Nimrod, as well as other Cold War jets, and an indoor space exploring the museum's varied collection of smaller displays including its Royal Air Force 100 Group Room and United States Army 8th Air Force Collection.

Combined Military Services Museum

Maldon, Essex, CM9 4LQ

Experience a journey through British military history, beginning on the brutal medieval battlefields, through the Crimean Napoleonic Wars and the First and Second World War to current-day conflicts. Learn about Special Forces, the Special Operations Executive and their daring operations.

The Gorse Industrial Estate

Thetford, Suffolk, IP24 2PH

Barnham Camp was a military establishment used during the First, Second and Cold Wars. Many of the structures, buildings and earthworks relating to the site still survive.

In the 1950s, it became a store for atomic bombs, and the pentagonal compound and structures associated with this phase of use are the most prominent survivors at the site.

Imperial War Museum, Duxford
Cambridge, CB22 4QR
Visit the Imperial War Museum Duxford for a huge day out. See Spitfires take to the skies from the airfield where they first flew, get up close to gigantic aircraft and walk in the footsteps of the men and women who served here. The extensive collections cover both military and civilian jets and are home to the American Air Museum and a collection of land warfare equipment.

Kelvedon Hatch Secret Nuclear Bunker
Brentwood, Essex, CM15 0LA
Come and witness the three lives of the bunker, starting with its role as an RAF ROTOR station and then a brief period as a civil defence centre through to its most recent life as a Regional Government HQ. Designed for up to 600 military and civilian personnel, their collective task was to organise the survival of the population in the awful aftermath of a nuclear war.

Landguard Fort
Felixstowe, Suffolk, IP11 3TW
The present Landguard fort is the last in a long line of defences built on the point protecting the natural harbour of Harwich. The fortification at Landguard was built to protect Harwich's deep-water harbour. During the Cold War, it was the Seaward Defence Headquarters with two 1950s casemates most likely intended to control all the gun batteries and shipping in the Harwich Harbour area and probably up as far as East Lane Battery at Bawdsey.

Langham Dome Museum
Holt, Norfolk, NR25 7BP
Langham Dome is one of only six remaining wartime gunnery centres that taught brave trainees how to shoot down enemy aircraft successfully. It offers a unique opportunity to journey back in time and experience what life was like for those who served at RAF Langham. The Langham Dome is the only one open to view as a museum.

The Muckleburgh Military Collection
Holt, Norfolk, NR25 7EH
The Muckleburgh Military Collection is Norfolk's largest working museum of military vehicles. It incorporates the Suffolk and Norfolk Yeomanry Museum of uniforms, weapons, photographs and documents, RAF Reconnaissance and Air Sea Rescue and Marine Craft.

Norfolk and Suffolk Aviation Museum
Bungay, Norfolk, NR35 1NZ
Late in 1972, a few local enthusiasts met and decided that steps should be taken to record something of the history of aviation in the Eastern counties and preserve aircraft and

artefacts. In May 1976, the museum was officially opened. Since then, the collection has grown from the occupation of the airfield by the 446th Bomb Group USAAF, followed briefly by the Fleet Air Arm and then the Royal Air Force, and aviation in the East of England.

Norfolk Tank Museum
Norwich, NR16 1HZ
The Norfolk Tank Museum houses a collection of military vehicles, weapons and militaria mainly from the twentieth century and the Cold War period. The collection of tanks and armoured cars is maintained in working condition or is awaiting restoration by the team. Other exhibits include artillery, uniforms, and an extensive collection of small British arms.

Orford Ness
Orford, Woodbridge, Suffolk, IP12 2NU
At Orford Ness, the largest vegetated shingle spit in Europe, a fascinating human history sits among an internationally important nature reserve. One of the earliest Royal Flying Corps airfields in Britain, Orford Ness was an important site for top-secret military testing from the First World War until the 1970s, including the early development of radar. As part of the Atomic Weapons Research Establishment after the Second World War, Orford Ness was involved with the development of Britain's nuclear deterrent, particularly the environmental testing of weapons. The built structures that survive from this period further contribute to the international significance of Orford Ness.

Peace Wood
Harlow Town Park, Harlow, Essex, CM20 2QQ
The core of the Town Park opened in 1957 and was unusual for the time in that conservation of the hamlet of Netteswell Cross, with its historic houses and eighteenth-century Greyhound pub took place. Landscaping included the infilling of seventeenth-century gravel pits, allowing an area of native woodland to develop. This was named Peace Wood in 1997 to mark the end of the Cold War.

RAF Coltishall Heritage Centre
RAF Coltishall, Norwich, NR10 5FB
Housed in the former Main Guardroom, the RAF Coltishall Heritage Centre is a project of the RAF Station Coltishall Heritage Trust. The trust has had no grant funding and relies on donations from supporters and visitors. The Heritage Centre exhibition rooms begin with the Battle of Britain and go through to the fast jets, including the Jaguar, the type that served the longest on this much-respected station.

The RAF Radar Museum (RAF Neatishead)
Horning, Norfolk, R12 8YB
Hidden within the peaceful surrounds of the Broads lies a clandestine world of air defence. RAF Neatishead, one of the oldest radar stations in the world, has been in operation since 1941. Housed in a Grade II listed 1942 operations building, the museum is a treasure

trove of stories, artefacts, and hands-on exhibits. The museum also boasts the UK's most complete Cold War-era Operations Room, which allows visitors the opportunity to step onto the front line of Britain's air defences.

Shoeburyness
Southend-on-Sea, Essex, SS3 9AB (Parking)
The concrete piles lying off the coast of south-east Essex are the remains of a defensive structure erected across the mouth of the River Thames. This 'boom' extended all the way to the other side of the water channel to Sheerness. In the early 1950s, a new boom was constructed to defend against the perceived threat from the Soviet Union but was obsolete on completion because of its uselessness against nuclear-armed bombers and missiles. In the 1960s, the boom at the Kent side was dismantled while that on the side of Essex is largely intact, although shortened by 600 meters to its current length of 2 km.

Stevenage Museum
Stevenage, Hertfordshire, SG1 1XX
Stevenage Museum is a small, family-friendly community museum telling the story of the town from pre-history to the modern day, including the evolution of Britain's first post-war new town. Across the road is the valiant 'nuclear-free zone', which the then council fought to establish in the town.

Wattisham Station Heritage Museum
Wattisham Airfield, Ipswich, Suffolk, IP7 7RA
The museum is housed in the original station chapel built by the USAAF in 1943. Inside the museum visitors see an extensive photographic record, artefacts, uniforms, equipment and memorabilia. Visitors are also able to see the Heritage Workshop located within a former Cold War Hardened Aircraft Shelter (HAS).

RAF Sculthorpe Heritage Centre
Wicken Green, Fakenham, NR21 7LX
The RAF Sculthorpe Heritage Centre tells the stories of the largest USAF atomic airbase outside the United States from 1947 to 1962. From the first Soviet Spyflights to heroes of the 1953 Floods,

An historic image from RAF Sculthorpe.

the RAF Sculthorpe Heritage Centre showcases the history of RAF Sculthorpe, the impact it made on the local community and tells the stories of the people that called Sculthorpe home.

North East

North East Land, Sea and Air Museums
Sunderland, SR5 3HZ

The North East Land Sea and Air Museum (NELSAM) sits on the former RAF Usworth and Sunderland airport site, next to the Sunderland Nissan factory, and comprises the former Aircraft Museum (NEAM), military vehicles collection, and the North East Electric Traction Trust (NEETT). The collections include a Cold War Avro Vulcan B2 bomber – the first Vulcan to go into private collection.

North West

Cecil Road Air-raid Siren
Cecil Road, Hale, Altrincham, WA15 9NX

The siren on Cecil Road was installed in 1938 and was one of 7,000 installed across the country in response to the threat of bombing by the Nazis. After the Second World War, the siren remained in use, this time in response to the threat of a nuclear attack during the Cold War. Unlike others, this one was not removed on the orders of the Home Office.

Imperial War Museum North
Trafford Park, Manchester, M17 1TZ

Situated in the heart of Salford Quays, the Imperial War Museum North is a striking building housing exhibitions dedicated to modern war and conflict. Focussing particularly on the impact of modern conflict on society, the Imperial War Museum North is one of five branches of the Imperial War Museum and the first to be located in the north of England.

Solway Aviation Museum
Carlisle Airport, CA6 4NW

The Solway Aviation Museum, based at Carlisle Airport, is home to a collection of aircraft and aviation artefacts and displays reflecting Britain's position as a world leader in aircraft design and innovation at the dawn of the jet age.

Yorkshire

Science and Media Museum
Pictureville, Bradford, BD1 1NQ

The National Science and Media Museum is a free museum in Bradford, West Yorkshire, devoted to the science and culture of light and sound technologies. The museum also hosts events for children and festivals covering animation, retro TV, film and more.

The York Bunker
Holgate, York, YO24 4HT

Operational from 1961, the group control in York was part of the UK's Warning and Monitoring Organisation (UKWMO). Staffed by volunteers from the Royal Observer

York Cold War Bunker. (© English Heritage)

Corps, the control collated data from around forty smaller bunkers across Yorkshire and the Humber to create a record of the location and power of nuclear detonations and subsequent fallout. Following stand-down in 1991, the control remained largely undisturbed until conservation work commenced in 2000. The site, opened to the public in 2006, presents one of the most complete and unaltered Cold War interiors within the UK.

Yorkshire Air Museum
Elvington, York, YO41 4AU
In 1952, RAF Elvington was handed over for use by the United States Air Force's Strategic Air Command. Major reconstruction began, which included lengthening and strengthening the runways to accept jet bomber aircraft as part of the Western Powers' nuclear deterrent. Today, the museum hosts a large collection of aircraft alongside historic buildings and museum spaces.

Scotland

Barnton Quarry
Clermiston Road North, Edinburgh, EH4 7BN
Located 4 miles from Edinburgh's city centre, the complex was developed for Britain's air defences during the Second World War and the subsequent Cold War. In the 1940s, phase one, built above ground, housed RAF Fighter Command Operations. Phase two, constructed from 1951 to 1953, integrated the RAF complex with a three-level ROTOR R4 SOC underground bunker. Obsolete by 1955, the complex accommodated civil defence administrations to prepare in the event of a nuclear attack. Surplus to requirements at the end of the Cold War in 1991, the complex was sold off, neglected, vandalised and in 1998, severely fire damaged by anarchists the Edinburgh Bomby Group. Since the mid-2000s, cleaning and structural restoration have been undertaken and may be viewed by arrangement. The ultimate ambition is to open the site as an exhibition space and a dedicated tourist attraction.

The Entrance to Barnton Quarry.

Dumfries Air Museum
Dumfries, DG1 3PH
Dumfries & Galloway Aviation Museum is a small independent museum passionate about the history of aviation and the local area. The museum has a collection of aircraft, including Battle of Britain veteran Loch Doon Spitfire, a supersonic Lightning fighter and a wartime assault glider collection.

Scotland's Secret Bunker
St Andrews, KY16 8QH
Hidden beneath an innocent Scottish farmhouse lies Scotland's Secret Bunker. A 450-foot tunnel leads you to the blast-proof doors that defend 24,000 square feet of secret accommodation, which was built to help safeguard Scotland during the Cold War in the event of a nuclear attack.

National Museum of Scotland
Chambers Street, Edinburgh, EH1 1JF
Explore the diversity of the natural world, world cultures, science and technology, art, design and fashion, and Scottish history, all under one roof. Collections include the Cold War.

National Museum of Flight
North Berwick, EH39 5LF
Discover a world-class collection of aircraft and hear the fascinating stories of the people who built and flew them at one of Scotland's top attractions. Learn about the history of aviation from the First World War to the present day and immerse yourself in interactive galleries and supersonic experiences.

Craigiebarns Bunker
Dundee, DD4 7GB
The bunker was opened in 1962 as the control bunker for the Royal Observer Corps' 28 (Dundee) Group. In 1976, it was extended in order to become the UK Warning and Monitoring Organisation (UKWMO) Caledonian Sector HQ bunker, taking over the role from the old site at School Hill and covering the whole of Scotland.

Gairloch Museum
Gairloch, IV21 2BH
In 2019, Gairloch Museum relocated to a stunning new building – a former nuclear bunker in the centre of Gairloch – and in 2020, it was named an Art Fund Museum of the Year.

Holy Loch
Sandbank, Dunoon, PA23 8PD
From 1961 to 1992, the loch was used as a United States Navy ballistic missile submarine base. This beautiful sea loch, which is situated in the Argyll Forest Park, has picturesque beaches, forest trails, and a stunning marina, which makes for a brilliant starting point for boating excursions.

Submarine Heritage Centre
Helensburgh, G84 8UN
Scotland's only submarine museum and education centre, based in Helensburgh, the home of the UK's Submarine fleet. The centre provides visitors with information about submarines and how they work.

Skelmorlie ROC Post
Skelmorlie, North Ayrshire, PA17 5HF
Skelmorlie is one of the very few restored Royal Observer Corps underground monitoring posts available for public access after the United Kingdom stand-down in September 1991 as a result of the ending of the Cold War.

Northern Ireland

Portadown Post
Portadown, BT62 1QU
Portadown teaches visitors about the Cold War and how a nuclear war would have affected the island of Ireland. It does not charge visitors an entrance fee and relies on donations to keep the museum totally free.

Other Organisations

Cold War Conversations
Cold War Conversations is an award-winning oral history project recording the real stories of the Cold War before they are lost. Every week, they interview an eyewitness to the Cold War. Across soldiers, spies, civilians, and others, they aim to cover the whole range of Cold War experiences. Host Ian Sanders brings your ears into the heart of the Cold War. Reading

THE AWARD WINNING

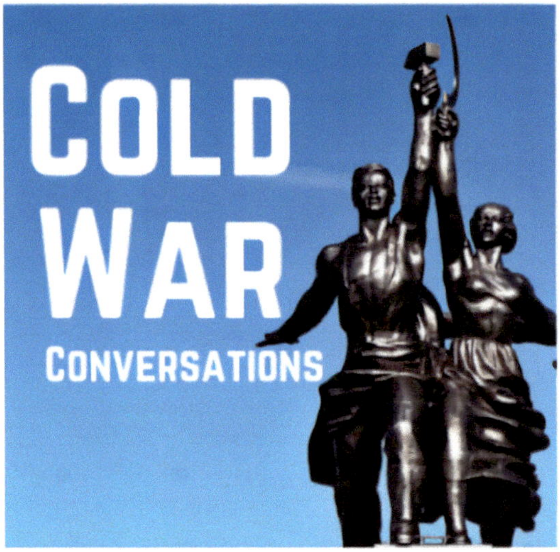

a history book is one thing, but hearing a human voice, with every breath, hesitation, and intonation, brings a whole new dimension to understanding what it was really like to be there.

The Military Vehicle Trust

Supports all people around the world interested in keeping ex-military vehicles of all kinds running and on the road. They have a growing membership of people, some of whom own vehicles and some who are just interested. Since 1978, the Military Vehicle Trust has provided help and support to members and members of the public, who have preserved thousands of military vehicles after their active lives with the armed forces. The trust sets out to achieve its charitable aims by promoting a huge range of activities that support members and advance public knowledge and understanding of how historic vehicles have contributed to our military heritage.

Cold War vehicles owned by members of The Military Vehicle Trust.